Skills for **Employability**

Step UP

Coursebook and **eBook**

B1

Linda Butler
Robyn Brinks Lockwood
Paul MacIntyre
Amy Renehan

Step Up B1

Pearson Education, 221 River Street, Hoboken, NJ 07030 USA

Cover Illustration: Roy Hermelin

Text composition: Straive

Library of Congress Cataloging-in-Publication Data: A catalog record for the print edition is available from the Library of Congress.

Printed in the United States of America

ISBN-13: 978-0-13-747357-1

1 2022

pearsonenglish.com/stepup

Acknowledgments

We would like to thank the following people for their help with this project.

Güzide Göksen Birol, Istanbul Okan University; **Eduardo Pinell Campuzano,** CIU Director, Universidad Privada Franz Tamayo; **Meg Cassamally,** University of Siena; **Adrian Crawley,** Evority Learning Centre; University of Siena; **Yabancı Diller,** School of Foreign Languages; **Louise Dixon,** Director of Studies at Hallo! Servizi Linguistici; **Aybala Eren,** Gazi University; **Alex Fayle,** Well & Will Language Academy; **Elizabeth Cruz Flores,** Tecnológico de Monterrey; **Jacques Friggieri,** Redrob; **María Amparo Garcia,** ICPNA Cusco; **Christina Gebbia,** Director of Let's Talk English Center in Valencia; **Maria de la Paz Giglio,** New Concept School of English; **Zeynep Güler,** İstanbul Okan University; **Ilaria Incorvaia,** ITIS 'Antonio Meucci', Florence; **Nancy Johnstone,** School of Engineering, UBA, Buenos Aires, Argentina; **Sevil Altıkulaçoğlu Kayaer,** Gazi University; **Yeliz Korkmaz,** Yıldız Technical University, Turkey; **Héctor Raúl Sánchez Lozano,** Proulex Universidad de Guadalajara; **Mariana Juana Aviles Martillo,** coordinator of CEFI, Center for Continuing Educatiòn and Interamerican Labor; **Anne Marie Mc Gowan,** University of Rome 'Tor Vergata' Italy; **Cristian Meléndez,** Universidad Católica de El Salvador; **Jose Manuel Mendivil S.,** Centro Boliviano Americano - Fundación Cultural y Educativa La Paz; **Paul Cruz Montenegro,** English Coordinator of CRC - Peru Cruceros; **M.Àngels Nogué,** Centre D'Idiomes Olot; **Irem Ozcan,** Gazi University, College of Foreign Languages; **Claudia Posarelli,** ITIS Meucci Firenze; **Steven Pragnell,** Astex Servicios Lingüísticos, Madrid; **María de Lourdes Camarillo Rodríguez,** Escuela Bancaria y Comercial; **Raquel Sánchez,** Faculty of Education in Albacete (UCLM); **Chayapak Tangapiwut,** Burapha University Language Institute; **Onur Uludag,** Yildiz Technical University; **Taku Umeda,** Tokyo Business and Language College; **Laura Vacca,** Inglese su Misura; **Marijke van Leuven,** Oxford School of English, Verona, Italy.

Photo Credits Page 2 (top): Gstockstudio/Shutterstock; 2 (1): MBI/Alamy Stock Photo; 2 (2): Bavorndej Prakit/123RF; 2 (3): Wavebreakmedia/Shutterstock; 2 (4): Dolgachov/123RF; 2 (5): Syda Productions/Shutterstock; 2 (6): Ammentorp/123RF; Shutterstock; 6: Marctran/123RF; 6 (web media icons): VectorForever/Shutterstock; 6 (social media icons): Rashad Ashur/Shutterstock; 6 (email icons): WonderfulPixel/Shutterstock; 6 (sad emoji): SpicyTruffel/Shutterstock; 7 (email icons): WonderfulPixel/Shutterstock; 7: Fizkes/123RF; 8 (mobile icons): Ico Maker/Shutterstock; 8: Rawpixel.com/Shutterstock; 9: PR Image Factory/Shutterstock; 10: Langstrup/123RF; 11 (left): Fizkes/123RF; 11 (right): Fizkes/123RF; 12 (left): Luis Molinero Martínez/123RF; 12 (right): Luis Molinero Martínez/123RF; 13: Ground Picture/Shutterstock; 14 (top): Mark Bowden/123RF; 14 (center): Seventyfour74/123RF; 14 (bottom): Wavebreak Media Ltd/123RF; 15: Shutterstock; 16: Red Deer/Shutterstock; 17 (left): Ollyy/Shutterstock; 17 (right): UfaBizPhoto/Shutterstock; 19 (top): Amelia Martin/123RF; 19 (center): Pixelheadphoto digitalskillet/Shutterstock; 19 (bottom): Rawpixel/123RF; 20: StockVector/Shutterstock; 21: Varandah/Shutterstock; 22 (left): Mark Bowden/123RF; 22 (right): Seventyfour74/123RF; 23 (left): Dmytro/123RF; 23 (right): LightField Studios/Shutterstock; 25: Fizkes/Shutterstock; 26: Evgeny Atamanenko/123RF; 27 (top): Rido/123RF; 27 (bottom): Iurii Golub/123RF; 29: Stokkete/123RF; 30: Wavebreak Media Ltd/123RF; 31: Lucky Business/Shutterstock; 32 (left, top): SofiaV/Shutterstock; 32 (left, center): Vectors Bang/Shutterstock; 32 (left, bottom): Iconic Bestiary/Shutterstock; 32 (right, top): RosyCre/Shutterstock; 32 (right, center): Sapann Design/Shutterstock; 32 (right, bottom): NotionPic/Shutterstock; 33: Rawpixel.com/Shutterstock; 34 (left): Victor4/123RF; 34 (right): Mark Bowden/123RF; 34 (mobile icons): Ico Maker/Shutterstock; 35 (left): Roman Rvachov/Shutterstock; 35 (left, center): Dolgachov/123RF; 35 (right, center): Flamingo Images/Shutterstock; 35(right): Syda Productions/Shutterstock; 36(top, left): Prostock-studio/Shutterstock; 36(top, center): Bbernard/Shutterstock; 36(top, right): Nd3000/123RF; 36 (bottom, left): Yakobchuk Viacheslav/Shutterstock; 36 (bottom, right): Weedezign/123RF; 37: Rawpixel/123RF; 38 (left): Seventyfour74/123RF; 38 (right): Instaphotos/123RF; 39: Seventyfour74/123RF; 40: Lisa Kolbasa/Shutterstock; 41 (left): Svitlana Sokolova/Shutterstock; 41 (left, center): Svitlana Sokolova/Shutterstock; 41 (right, center): Svitlana Sokolova/Shutterstock; 41 (right): Svitlana Sokolova/Shutterstock; 42 (left): The Picture Art Collection/Alamy Stock Photo; 42 (right): Armando Arorizo/Prensa Internacional/ZUMA Press, Inc./Alamy Stock Photo; 43: Lyudmyla Kharlamova/123RF; 44: Venimo/Shutterstock; 45: Rawpixel/123RF; 46 (top): Dinis Tolipov/123RF; 46 (bottom): Mark Bowden/123RF; 47: MF production/Shutterstock; 49: Prostock-studio/Shutterstock; 50 (left): George Rudy/Shutterstock; 50 (right): Daniel Ernst/123RF; 52: Alexander Lysenko/Shutterstock.

Scope and Sequence

Welcome page 2	In the classroom | Learn about your book | Meet your Employability Skills Coaches

Module	I can . . .	Learning Objectives	Vocabulary
1 **Communication 1** Interpersonal Communication Skills pages 5–8	I can explain the importance of having good interpersonal communication skills.	• Identify strong and weak interpersonal communication skills • Describe specific strategies for making a good first impression • Describe specific strategies for communicating information and instructions clearly • Describe specific strategies for giving and receiving negative feedback	*approachable, criterion, criticism, defensive, employability, impression, misunderstanding, motivated, respectful, tone*
2 **Communication 2** Handling Difficult Situations pages 9–12	I can describe specific strategies for effectively handling difficult situations at work.	• Identify strong communication skills for handling difficult situations at work • Identify communication mistakes • Describe specific strategies for dealing with customer problems	*concerned, command, deal with, guidelines, identify, interaction, resolve, respectfully, successfully*
3 **Goal Setting** Short- and Long-Term SMART Goals pages 13–16	I can explain the importance of setting SMART goals.	• Define the SMART method • Describe the relationship between short- and long-term goals • Distinguish short- from long-term goals • Identify strong and weak goal statements	*accomplish, achievable, consideration, long-term goal, measurable, milestone, relatively, relevant, short-term goal, time-bound*
4 **Teamwork** Key Attributes of Teamwork pages 17–20	I can explain the importance of teamwork and describe the characteristics of an effective team.	• Describe key characteristics of an effective team • Identify specific strategies for improving teamwork and collaboration	*achieve, authority, characteristic, collaborate, continuous, credit, effective, facilitate, responsibility, structure*
5 **Critical Thinking** Perspective Taking pages 21–24	I can explain the importance of perspective taking in the workplace.	• Define perspective taking • Describe the benefits of perspective taking • Describe specific strategies for understanding different perspectives	*analyze, beneficial, compromise, creative, crucial, disagreement, diverse, frustrating, personality, perspective, values*
6 **Leadership** Leading a Group pages 25–28	I can explain the importance of leadership skills and describe specific leadership strategies.	• Identify leadership skills • Describe qualities and behaviors of a good leader • Describe specific strategies for leading groups of people	*acknowledge, come up with, encourage, inspire, promotion, role model, supervision, take a risk, vision, vital*

Pronunciation	Language Strategy	Project	Talk!
Stressed syllables	Recognize and understand contrastive stress	Ask the four questions about interpersonal communication to a good communicator	How technology is changing the ways we communicate
Silent letters	Summarize explanations or instructions	Search for common workplace communication problems and tips to deal with them	Communication problems in the workplace or at school
Sounds /ɚ/ and /ɔr/	Listen for instructions	Interview a person about a long-term goal and the steps they took to achieve it	The importance of short- and long-term SMART goals in achieving success
Compound nouns	Take notes with symbols and abbreviations	Research different online collaboration tools and choose one that is the most helpful to you	Facts about teamwork
Simple present *-s* endings	Listen for enumeration	Interview two to three people about their experiences with perspective taking	The importance of perspective taking
Weak pronunciation of object pronouns	Recognize and understand definitions	Interview someone who has a leadership role	Choose the best quote and explain why

Module	I can . . .	Learning Objectives	Vocabulary
7 **Self-Management** Time Logs pages 29–32	I can describe specific strategies for improving my time management skills.	• Identify common time management problems • Recall specific strategies for solving time management problems • Describe the benefits of keeping a time log	*accountable, agenda, correspond, efficient, essential, estimate, interrupt, overestimate, priority, productivity, rule of thumb, underestimate*
8 **Wellness** Balancing Your Wellness Dimensions pages 33–36	I can describe the dimensions of wellness and strategies for improving wellness.	• Describe five dimensions of wellness • Identify weak and strong areas of wellness • Describe specific strategies for improving wellness	*assess, balance, dimension, emotional, fulfillment, intellectual, isolated, mutual, nutritious, spiritual, strengthen, workload*
9 **Social Responsibility** Diversity and Inclusion pages 37–40	I can explain the importance of diversity and inclusion in the workplace.	• Define diversity and inclusion • Describe the benefits of having a diverse and inclusive work environment • Describe specific strategies for implementing diversity and inclusion in the workplace	*acceptance, discrimination, executive, implement, innovative, intolerance, mission, promote, strategy, synergy*
10 **Branding** Building Your Personal Brand pages 41–44	I can explain the importance of personal branding and describe strategies for building my brand.	• Describe the components of a personal brand • Describe specific strategies for building a personal brand • Describe specific strategies for representing a personal brand in a résumé and online	*ambitious, authentic, combination, competitive, expertise, stand out, suitability, unique*
11 **Job Search** How to Build a Network pages 45–48	I can explain the importance of networking and describe strategies for building my network.	• Define networking • Describe specific strategies to build an online network • Describe specific strategies to improve networking IRL	*contacts, enhance, expand, graduate, keep in touch, make small talk, network, profile, recommendation, reputation, virtual*
12 **Interviewing** Preparing for an Interview pages 49–52	I can describe specific strategies for improving my interview skills.	• Describe specific tips and strategies for preparing for an interview • Identify appropriate responses to common interview questions • Describe specific strategies for following-up after an interview	*background, candidate, confidence, factor, illegal, impatient, qualifications, references, relevant, unrelated*

Pronunciation	Language Strategy	Project	Talk!
Simple past *-ed* endings	Listen for key words and phrases	Research common time management mistakes	Time management personality types
Voiceless */th/* sound	Recognize and understand signal words and phrases	Choose one of the dimensions of wellness and create additional tips for how to improve this dimension	Unusual wellness ideas in the workplace
Linking vowel-vowel	Listen for numbers	Research what companies do to promote diversity and inclusion in the workplace	Compare different icebreaker activities to build an inclusive environment
Thought groups	Scan for details using keywords	Present your brand and explain how it makes you stand out	The importance of your online presence and personal branding
Consonant groups	Identify examples as supporting details	Research different sites that are for online professional networking	Different ideas for networking events and activities
Sounds and spelling for vowel /aɪ/, /ɪ/, and /i/	Interview skill: Buying time	Search online for common interview questions and find recommendations on how to answer them	Rank common job interview mistakes

To the Teacher

Overview

Step Up is a flexible online course designed for adults or young adults who want to improve their employability skills—whether to get a first job, secure a promotion, find a different job, re-enter the workforce after an absence, or change fields. Although the emphasis of the course is on employability skills, *Step Up* also develops English language skills by providing vocabulary instruction and practice, listening, reading, and notetaking skills, pronunciation practice, and discussion strategies.

Levels

There are six levels of *Step Up*, CEFR A2+ to C1, Global Scale of English (GSE) 34 to 84.

***Step Up* level**	**GSE**
Step Up A2+	34–43
Step Up B1	41–51
Step Up B1+	49–58
Step Up B2	56–66
Step Up B2+	64–75
Step Up C1	73–84

Two Versions of *Step Up*

Students can study the *Step Up* course in two ways: as a self-study course or as a self-study plus course, which is the self-study course combined with a teacher-led class. As a self-study course, each level of *Step Up* takes students 18 hours to complete, though this may vary as it is self-paced. The teacher-led course provides 14 hours of class time, with additional resources and extension activities available in the Teaching Notes, which would extend class time.

Student's Components

	Self-study course	**Self-study plus course**
Online Course	✓	✓
Coursebook + eBook or eBook only	✗	✓
Resources (online)	✓	✓

Teacher's Components

	Self-study plus course
Coursebook and/or eBook	✓
Access to the Online Course	✓
Teaching Notes	✓
Resources (online)	✓

The Online Course

Students study the following 12 modules, of which the first nine are **personal and social capabilities** and the last three are job-seeking skills:

Module 1 Communication 1	**Module 2** Communication 2	**Module 3** Goal Setting
Module 4 Teamwork	**Module 5** Critical Thinking	**Module 6** Leadership
Module 7 Self-Management	**Module 8** Wellness	**Module 9** Social Responsibility
Module 10 Job Search	**Module 11** Branding	**Module 12** Interviewing

Each module has an employability skills coach—an animated character—who takes the students through the 10 steps of the module. Step 11 is a progress check; it includes a practice test and a graded test. If the student scores at least 70% on every graded test, they are given access to the final exam. If they score at least 80% on this assessment, they receive a certificate of completion.

For a closer look at the online course, please see the Online Module Walkthrough in the Teacher Resources.

Coursebook/eBook

The Coursebook/eBook is made up of two main sections: the modules and the back matter.

The Modules

Welcome Module

The Coursebook begins with a Welcome Module, which is comprised of four sections to:

- help students get to know each other and form a community of learners
- provide students with useful language they need to work effectively in class
- help students navigate the Coursebook so they get the most out of it
- introduce students to the 12 employability skills coaches they meet in the online course.

The 12 Employability Skills Modules

Following the Welcome Module are the 12 employability skills modules, corresponding to each module in the online course. Students need to do each online module before they come to class. In class, you guide them through each module to reinforce what they have learned online, to deepen their understanding of the material, and to share how they can apply what they have learned to their own lives.

Back Matter

There are four sections in the back of the Coursebook and eBook:

- *Check your understanding* enables students to demonstrate they have understood the material they have studied online and gives them an opportunity to clear up any misunderstandings at the beginning of a class.
- *Discussion strategies* provide students with four different sets of strategies that can help them engage in class. These include how to work with others; clarify what you hear or clarify what you say; get and stay involved in the discussion; and organize your ideas. Audio models enable students to practice their pronunciation.
- *Vocabulary practice* gives students additional practice with the vocabulary they have learned in the online course. The first activity is a word puzzle, and the second activity uses the target words from the puzzle in context. The answers are provided in the eBook and in the Resources folder.
- *The Glossary* provides the definitions of some words or phrases printed in light brown in the Coursebook to facilitate understanding.

Flexibility

While the sequence of the modules is fixed in the coursebook, you can change the sequence to meet the needs of your students. You may want to have the class review the scope and sequence and vote on which modules to do first. If you change the sequence, we suggest you create a syllabus and upload it to the platform.

Resources for Students

All audio and video files for the online course and all audio files for the coursebook are accessible within the activities in the course. In addition, these audio and video files are also available in the Resources, to allow students to watch or listen whenever they wish without going to the lesson itself. Also included in the Resources are the reading texts, as well as answer keys to the *Vocabulary practice* in the Coursebook.

Resources for Teachers

Teaching Notes

There are general teaching notes to help you get the most out of the course. Then there are notes for each module that begin with an overview of the online module that synopsizes what the students have learned online. Following the overview are teaching notes for each step in the coursebook, including tips, extensions, culture notes, and more.

Module Walkthroughs

There is also a module walkthrough that visually describes a module and the underlying pedagogy for both the online course and the coursebook.

Platform Support

To help you navigate the platform and use all the tools available, there is a guided tour when you first log on to Pearson English Connect. In addition, you will find numerous resources under the "Help" button to orient you to the platform. And to get in touch with support, you can click on Help>Documentation>Contact Support.

Welcome

1 In the classroom

A Get to know your classmates

Say your name and one thing about yourself. Repeat what your classmates said.

B Useful language

Complete the conversations with sentences from the box. Then listen and check your answers.

a	~~What was that last part again?~~	**e**	Could you explain that a bit more?
b	Could you speak up, please?	**f**	How do you say "firma" in English?
c	What's the difference between "I want" and "I would like"?		
d	you're saying we should interview our partners and take notes?		

C Role play

PAIRS Choose a conversation from 1B and role play it. Use different information.

② Learn about your book

1 How many modules are in the course?

a 5 **b** 9 **c** 11 **d** 12

2 How many steps are in each module?

a 6 **b** 7 **c** 8 **d** 9

3 Look at this icon on page 5. It tells you to go to page 68. Read what is on that page. How can you use that information?

DISCUSSION STRATEGIES

Go to page 68.

____

4 On page 5, Exercise C says Check your understanding. Go to page 54. What is on that page?

a questions to test vocabulary
b questions to ask my teacher
c questions to review the Online Course
d questions to ask my partner

5 Look through Module 1. Which Steps in the book refer to Steps in the Online Course?

a Steps 1, 2, and 3
b Steps 2, 5, and 7
c Steps 3, 4, and 6
d Steps 5, 6, and 7

6 Look at the I-can statement after Step 7 in each module, for example

I can identify successful communication skills. ☐

What is it for?

____

7 What will you find on pages 72–83?

a listening practice
b grammar practice
c vocabulary practice
d pronunciation practice

8 What will you find on pages 86–87?

a a glossary
b listening activities
c vocabulary practice
d an audio script

To find the answers for CHECK YOUR UNDERSTANDING and VOCABULARY PRACTICE you can look in your ebook or use the answer key in the Student's Resources online.

Meet your Employability Skills Coaches

MODULE 1
Greetings! I'm Dr. Jabu Cele. I have my doctorate in communications and I'm a senior vice president at one of the world's top marketing companies.

MODULE 2
Hi there! I'm Emma Lu, and I'll be your coach for the Communication 2 module. I'm a corporate teamwork coach.

MODULE 3
Hello there. I'm Zehra Teke and I'll be your Employability Skills coach for the module about Goal Setting. I'm a business consultant with a master's degree in management.

MODULE 4
Hello! My name is Kristine Ross. I'm the human resources manager for a large, international company. I'll be your coach for the Teamwork module.

MODULE 5
Hello. My name is Marek Kamiński. I'm an investigative journalist and I'll be your Employability Skills coach for the Critical Thinking module.

MODULE 6
Hi, I'm Sonia Lopez. I'll be your coach for the Leadership module. I'm the Chief Executive Officer—the CEO—of the Alacarte Restaurant Group.

MODULE 7
Hello, my name is Felix Becker. I'm a professional certified life coach and I'll be your coach for the Self-Management module.

MODULE 8
Hello and welcome to the Wellness module. I'll be your Employability Skills coach. My name is Kai Sugimoto. I have a PhD in psychology and I do research on health and wellness.

MODULE 9
Hello, there. My name is Ana Silva. I'm the coordinator of social responsibilty for a large company and I am your coach for the Social Responsibilty module.

MODULE 10
Hi. Welcome to the Branding module. I'm Rakesh Patel, and I'm your Employability Skills coach. I work in marketing.

MODULE 11
Hello! Welcome. I'm Justin Roy, and I'm your coach for the Job Search module. I'm a career advice blogger and my goal is to help people find their dream jobs.

MODULE 12
Hi. My name is Aisha Omar. I'm a career counselor at the U.S. Department of Labor and I'll be your coach for the Interviewing module.

1 MODULE

Communication 1

Interpersonal Communication Skills

DISCUSSION STRATEGIES

Go to page 68.

Step 1 Get started

A Refresh your memory! Watch the *What You'll Learn* video.

B Look at the photo. In what different ways are people communicating? What communication problems may they have?

C Check your understanding. Go to page 54.

Step 2 Tell your story

A THINK In your online course, you thought about a time that you had to communicate for work, school, or in your personal life. What happened and what did you learn? Listen to the example.

B PAIRS Discuss your story.

C SHARE Tell your story to the class.

Step 3 Activate your knowledge

A PAIRS Read the scenarios below that show people communicating in different situations. Discuss how the people are using their interpersonal skills to communicate and write tips for improvement.

1 Read the post written by Zane, a team leader, on a company's website where employees can ask for advice. What could Zane and his team do to improve their communication during online meetings? Take notes.

I've always liked face-to-face meetings at work. I use a lot of body language and gestures, and I'm good at turn-taking, so my conversations go very smoothly.

Recently, however, I have started running virtual meetings for my team, and things aren't going so well. There are long pauses and it's difficult to know when someone is finished talking or someone else wants to say something, so we're constantly interrupting each other. Also, after every meeting, I'm finding that many people still have questions that they didn't have a chance to ask during the meeting. It also bothers me and others when people just get up and leave their desks without saying anything or when they turn off their cameras and we can't see their faces. I think this is bad for the atmosphere—you know, how the team members feel about the meeting.

I really miss face-to-face meetings because everyone got to know each other. Now everyone is feeling anxious and uncomfortable because it's difficult to communicate, and there's really no chance to become friendly with colleagues.

2 Read the email sent to employees and the reply below. What did the writers of these emails do wrong? How could they improve their written communication? Take notes.

TO: All Staff
SUBJECT: Email to Staff

We're fast approaching March 31, and a lot of you STILL haven't submitted your expense reports or selected your vacation days, and I also noticed that several people haven't completed their performance reviews (THIS MEANS YOU MARK AND AUDRA!), and some haven't submitted office supply requests, and it's also time to make your meeting room reservations for next month, and tell us if you plan to donate to the office charity fund. **GET THESE THINGS DONE!** ☹

Emma,
Acting Office Manager

TO: Emma Hicks
SUBJECT:

Hello Emma,
Just a quik note to let you know that I've put together my expense report and am planing to submit it by friday. Thanks for the reminder, though. You remind me of an elephant, Emma—because you never forget! LOL

Best regards,
Audra Bean

3 Read and listen to the beginning of a performance interview. What did the manager and Charles, the employee, do well? What could they have done better? Take notes.

Manager: Thanks for coming, Charles. I'll be honest with you. I've done twenty performance reviews a day for the last four days, so I'm sorry if I seem a little stressed.
Charles: I see. Thanks for letting me know.
Manager: First of all, I'd like to thank you for the great work your team did last year. However, it seems the quality of work from your team isn't as high as last year.
Charles: Really? I'm surprised to hear that. According to what criteria?
Manager: It seems clear enough from the customer feedback we've been getting. Can you think of any reasons that your team might be receiving this kind of feedback? Are there any issues you'd like to share with me?
Charles: Are you sure it isn't that new customer feedback form? The questions are pretty confusing. I really don't feel anything about our work has changed.
Manager: We're sure the problem isn't with the form.
Charles: Well, it might be the new employee, William. He's still learning things.
Manager: As team leader, your role is to make sure all the members of your team are taking responsibility for and sharing the team's success.
Charles: Thanks for reminding me of that. Perhaps I need to call a meeting and make sure everyone clearly understands their role as team members.

B SHARE Present your answers to the class. Take notes while other pairs share their answers.

Step 4 Take away

GROUPS of 3–5 Create a diagram and write the interpersonal communication tips from your answers in Step 3 as well as the ones you learned from your classmates. Include four categories, one for each question from the module.

Interpersonal communication tips

Are you creating the right impression?
Ask for clarification if needed.

Are you communicating information effectively?

Do you give instructions politely and clearly?

How do you give and take feedback?

Step 5 Project

PAIRS **In your online course, you asked the four questions about interpersonal communication to someone you know who is a good communicator. Share their answers with your partner. Discuss which of the answers were the most interesting and useful and add them to the diagram in Step 4. Read the example.**

I interviewed one of my colleagues at work. I think she's especially effective in meetings. In answer to the question—How do you create the right impression?—she said being positive and putting yourself in the other person's position were the two most important guidelines to remember.

Step 6 Talk!

GROUPS of 3–4 **As technology makes communication easier and faster than ever before, personal communication is becoming less formal. Discuss how technology is changing the ways we communicate. Use the facts and questions to help guide your conversation.**

Over 68% of people prefer to text than make calls in their personal lives.

A recent survey found that 61% of employees use emojis in their emails at work.

Consumers in Asia and the US prefer text messaging to voice calls when they communicate with customer service teams.

3.5 million business and personal emails are sent every second, but only about a third are opened, and 8.5% receive a reply.

- Should informal communication be more accepted in the business world?
- In what situations is using emojis and informal language in the workplace acceptable?
- If people prefer to use written communication when they contact customer service, should companies get rid of phone customer service altogether?
- If the new trends in communication continue, what do you think workplace communication will look like ten years from now? What about fifty years from now?

Step 7 Going forward

A **PAIRS** **In your online course, you reflected on which types of situations you will handle differently after studying more about interpersonal communication skills. Discuss. Listen to the example.**

B **SHARE** **Present your ideas to the class.**

VOCABULARY PRACTICE
Go to page 72.

I can explain the importance of having good interpersonal communication skills. ☐

2

MODULE

Communication 2

Handling Difficult Situations

DISCUSSION STRATEGIES

Go to page 68.

Step 1 Get started

A Refresh your memory! Watch the *What You'll Learn* video.

B Look at the photo. What do you think is happening? How would you handle this type of situation if you were the clerk?

C Check your understanding. Go to page 55.

Step 2 Tell your story

A THINK In your online course, you thought about a problem you had at work, school, or in your personal life involving communication. What caused the problem and what happened? Listen to the example.

B PAIRS Discuss your story.

C SHARE Tell your story to the class.

Step 3 Take away

A PAIRS Review your notes from the online module and complete the communication guidelines. Use one word in each gap.

Follow up	respectful	plan	commands	Listen	Summarize	solve	defensive

Communication guidelines for handling difficult situations

1 ________________ carefully.
2 Try not to seem ________________.
3 Be ________________ and not too casual.
4 Use polite questions instead of ________________.
5 ________________ your understanding of the problem.
6 Explain your ________________ for fixing the problem.
7 Work to ________________ the issue.
8 ________________ with the customer.

B SHARE Check your answers with the class.

Step 4 Activate your knowledge

A PAIRS Listen to a conversation between co-workers. Pay attention to how each person communicates. Did they both follow the communication guidelines? What did they do correctly or incorrectly? Take notes.

B PAIRS Choose one of the role-play scenarios. Student A: You are the manager. Student B: You are the employee. Study your card and perform the role play with your partner using your own ideas and the communication guidelines from Step 3. Then discuss and take notes on how well you handled the situation and what you could have done differently.

ROLE PLAY 1

Student A

You are a manager at a small company that sells software to other companies. You need to talk to an employee about customer complaints you have received.

- *Recently several customers have had problems with your software. You received complaints that a member of your support staff has not done enough to help the clients.*
- *It is the company rule to report all problems to the manager, but the employee has not done that.*
- *The employee has joined the team only recently and you think that maybe he or she needs more training.*
- *Customer complaints make you stressed because you are a small company and customer satisfaction is very important.*

Student B

You are an employee at a company that sells software to other companies. Your manager is going to talk to you about customer complaints.

- *You are a new member of the support staff, and your job is to take care of the problems reported by the customers.*
- *The latest problem does not seem very serious, but you do not know how to solve it. You have had so much work lately that you have not asked anyone for help yet.*
- *Your manager seemed stressed out lately. You did not want to worry her or him with the problem, so you have not reported it.*

ROLE PLAY 2

Student A

You are the owner of a popular restaurant. You need to talk to an employee about customer complaints you have received.

- *You have received complaints from several guests that one of the servers got their orders wrong and was rude when they discovered the mistake.*
- *You are surprised because the employee is very experienced and has always done his or her job well.*
- *You have trained your servers to always be polite and avoid conflicts with guests. Customer satisfaction is very important for you because your business depends on guest reviews.*

Student B

You are an employee at a popular restaurant. Your boss is going to talk to you about customer complaints.

- *You have been working as a server for several years and you like your job.*
- *Recently you have been working in the evenings and on weekends when the restaurant is very busy, so you are often tired and overworked.*
- *You remember serving a large group of guests who changed their order several times. When you served their food, they said they had wanted something else and blamed you for their mistakes.*
- *You feel that your boss does not always take the time to fully understand the situation or listen to employees.*

C SHARE Present your comments and ideas to the class. Listen to other students and add their ideas to your notes.

Step 5 Project

GROUPS of 3–5 **In your online course, you searched the internet for common workplace communication problems and tips on how to deal with them. Share the problems and the tips you found with your group. Read the example.**

I read about active listening. Everyone knows that active listening is important, but one common problem I found is that managers sometimes forget that this applies to them. What happens then is that employees feel that their needs and problems are ignored. This affects their motivation and engagement. One of the tips for employees is to follow up with their manager to make sure they work together to solve the issue.

Step 6 Talk!

PAIRS **Communication problems in the workplace or at school happen to everyone. They could lead to funny or embarrassing situations. Talk about communication problems in the workplace or at school. Use the questions to help guide your conversation.**

- Think about movies or TV shows set in the workplace or at school. What are some funny situations you remember happening that relate to communication?
- We have all had difficult or embarrassing communication problems with people at work or school. What are some situations that have happened to you with a boss, colleague, teacher, or classmate?

I was really tired at work the other day and as I was leaving I said, "Bye! I love you!" to my BOSS! I'm so used to saying that to my kids when I leave the house, I just said it without thinking. I was SO embarrassed!"

After a busy week at work, I was excited about the weekend. I saw one of the guys in my office leaving early for the day and I shouted, "Have a great weekend!" He said nothing and just gave me a strange look. Then I found out he had been fired and was leaving the office forever.

Step 7 Going forward

A **PAIRS** **In your online course, you reflected on how you would handle difficult situations differently using your communication skills. Discuss. Listen to the example.**

B **SHARE** **Present your ideas to the class.**

VOCABULARY PRACTICE Go to page 73.

I can describe specific strategies for effectively handling difficult situations at work. ☐

3
MODULE

Goal Setting

Short- and Long-Term SMART Goals

DISCUSSION STRATEGIES

Go to page 68.

Step 1 Get started

A Refresh your memory! Watch the *What You'll Learn* video.

B Look at the photo. These people have just achieved their goal of graduating from university. What may their next long-term goal be and what short-term goals do they need to achieve it?

C Check your understanding. Go to page 56.

Step 2 Tell your story

A THINK In your online course, you thought about a long-term goal you have achieved at work, school, or in your personal life. How did you plan for it and finally achieve it? What short-term goals did you set for yourself along the way? Listen to the example.

B PAIRS Discuss your story.

C SHARE Tell your story to the class.

Step 3 Activate your knowledge

A PAIRS Read about these long-term goals. Suggest short-term goals that could help to achieve them in the chart below. Include details that would make the goals SMART.

SMART goals:
- specific
- measurable
- achievable
- relevant
- time-bound

1

Trent
I've been working as a healthcare assistant for a few years now. I really like it. I like helping people and I think that I'm very good at my job. But now I'm ready for a change. I'd really like to go to nursing school within the year so I can become a nurse, but I don't know which nursing program to apply to. I also have to find out how much it costs and if I can work while I'm studying.

2

Kayla
I started as a warehouse worker in a large manufacturing company two months ago. I know this is a good job, but I think I can do other jobs in this company. I have a high school diploma, excellent analytical skills, and I also know a lot about quality control. I don't think a certificate is necessary to work as a quality control inspector. Anyway, I'd like to find another position in this company in the next six months.

3

Jordan
I own a small house-painting business with two employees and one van. Right now, I mostly get work when happy customers recommend me to their friends and families. I really want to double the size of my business over the next year. I've been very successful, so I know I have enough money to advertise and grow. But I'm not very good at marketing and I don't know where to start.

4 **Jasmine**
I've been working in sales for several years, but I don't really enjoy it anymore. That's why I've decided to change careers. I have a degree in math, and I love working with young people, so I want to be a high school teacher. I make a good salary now, so the new job will mean a pay cut, but I'm ready for that. However, I'm not sure where to start.

	Long-term goal	Short-term goals
Trent		
Kayla		
Jordan		
Jasmine		

B SHARE Compare you ideas with another pair's and choose the best short-term goals for each person.

Step 4 Take away

A PAIRS Think of a SMART long-term goal for yourself. Then work with a partner to write short-term goals to support your long-term goal. Take notes in the chart. Add more short-term goals if necessary.

Short-term goal	→	Short-term goal	→	Short-term goal	→	Long-term goal

B SHARE Present your goals to another pair. Take notes while others are presenting theirs and give each other feedback.

Step 5 Project

PAIRS **In your online course, you interviewed someone you know who is successful and asked them about a big goal they have accomplished and the steps they had to take to achieve this goal. Present the information you learned to your partner. Read the example.**

My friend loves cooking and last year she decided to start her own food truck business. Her first goal was to get the money for the truck by delivering lunches to offices. To do that, she went downtown with samples of food to give out, to see if people liked it. They did, so she started taking orders and after a few months had enough money for the truck. Next, she had to get licenses needed to start the business.

Step 6 Talk!

PAIRS **Setting goals helps make progress in many areas of life. Discuss the importance of short- and long-term SMART goals in achieving success. Use the questions and facts to help guide your conversation.**

- How far ahead do you feel comfortable planning?
- When a goal is difficult to achieve, do you give up or improve it and try again? Why?
- Is setting goals always necessary? Do you think it's easier to live life without setting goals and just live for the moment?

14% of people set goals but never write them down.

Only 3% of people keep a written list of goals.

People with written goals are three times more likely to achieve success than those with unwritten goals.

83% of adults do not have goals.

Most big goals usually take people between five to ten years to achieve.

Reviewing goals regularly helps to keep them relevant and achievable.

Step 7 Going forward

A **PAIRS** **In your online course, you reflected on which types of situations in your life you will handle differently after studying about setting goals. Discuss. Listen to the example.**

B **SHARE** **Present your ideas to the class.**

VOCABULARY PRACTICE
Go to page 74.

I can explain the importance of setting SMART goals. ☐

4

MODULE

Teamwork

Key Attributes of Teamwork

DISCUSSION STRATEGIES

Go to page 68.

Step 1 Get started

A Refresh your memory! Watch the *What You'll Learn* video.

B Look at the photos. What do these two different teams have in common?

C Check your understanding. Go to page 57.

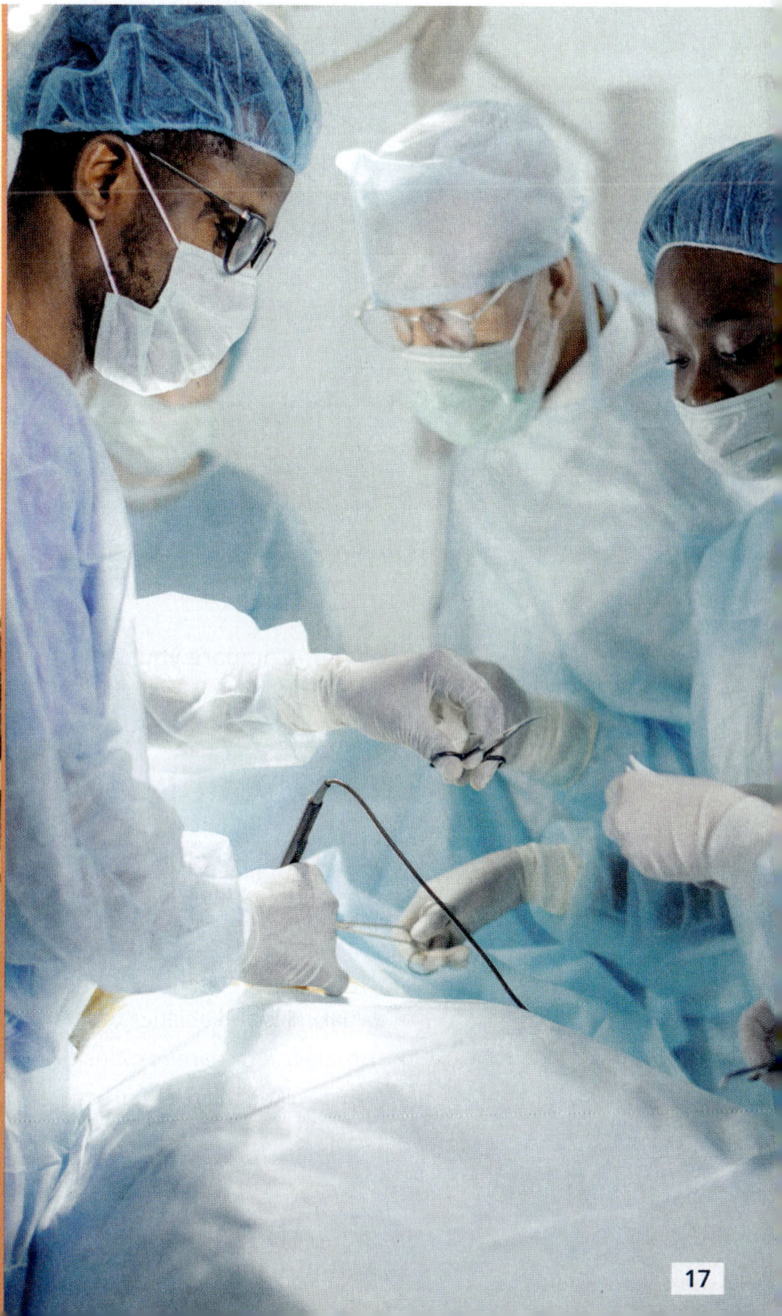

Step 2 Tell your story

A THINK In your online course, you thought about a time that you were a member of a team at work, school, or in your personal life. How did you work together to achieve your goal? Listen to the example.

B PAIRS Discuss your story.

C SHARE Tell your story to the class.

Step 3 Take away

A PAIRS Review your notes from the online module and explain the key characteristics of an effective team.

Key team characteristics	Explanation
a shared goal	*Effective teams have a common goal that all team members agree on, understand, and work toward.*
continuous communication	
collaboration	
shared responsibility and authority	
a clear team structure	

B SHARE Compare your answers with another pair's.

Step 4 Activate your knowledge

A GROUPS Read the scenarios. Discuss how you will work together as a team to achieve each goal. Use the key team characteristics from Step 3 and these questions to guide you. Take notes.

- How will your team communicate before, during, and after the event?
- What skills and abilities of team members will help your team achieve the goal?
- How will you share responsibility and authority?
- What will be the team structure and the roles and responsibilities of team members?

1

Fundraising event

Your company wants to raise money for a new community garden that will open in the spring. Your team has volunteered to organize a bake sale as a fundraising event in the office. You plan to donate homemade cakes, cookies, pies, and other snacks, and to sell these in the office lunchroom. The bake sale has been planned for one day. The company will provide money to help organize the event.

____

____

2

Career fair

Your employer has asked your team to represent the company at a job fair. The HR department will organize training for you before the event. You will have a booth to display the information about your company. You will need to talk about the company, answer questions, and hand out materials. Your task is to identify people interested in working for the company and get their contact information. The fair will be six hours.

____

____

3

Farewell party

One of your coworkers, Ana, is changing jobs and leaving the company in three weeks. Your team has agreed to organize a surprise farewell party on her last day at work. All twenty colleagues from the office are invited. A nearby restaurant is the perfect place for the party. Your boss has given you a budget to pay for the food and drinks. You would like everyone to chip in so that you can get a farewell gift for Ana from all of you.

____

____

B SHARE **Talk about how each team plans to work. Take notes and give each other feedback.**

Step 5 Project

GROUPS of 3–5 In your online course, you researched online collaboration tools and chose one or two that you thought were the most helpful. Present the results of your research to the group. Read the example.

One tool I found is Wimi. Wimi has a lot of great features that help teams to communicate and collaborate on projects online. It allows team members to organize tasks, share schedules and files, and have discussions and meetings—all this without having to install anything on your computer. It keeps everything in one place, and it makes sure users always have the most recent information and files.

Step 6 Talk!

PAIRS Many situations in the workplace require collaborating with others on a team. Read the facts about teamwork. Discuss each one. Are you surprised by these facts?

Employees spend 50% more time collaborating compared to five years ago.

Working in teams is important for 75% of workers.

Teams made up of members who always think alike are not very creative or innovative.

70% of employees feel that digital technology makes collaboration and teamwork easier.

Step 7 Going forward

A PAIRS In your online course, you reflected on how your participation in situations that require teamwork will change after studying more about teamwork skills. Discuss. Listen to the example.

B SHARE Present your ideas to the class.

VOCABULARY PRACTICE Go to page 75.

I can explain the importance of teamwork and describe the characteristics of an effective team. ☐

5 MODULE

Critical Thinking

Perspective Taking

DISCUSSION STRATEGIES
Go to page 68.

Step 1 Get started

A Refresh your memory! Watch the *What You'll Learn* video.

B Look at the photo. Perspective taking is compared to wearing different "hats." When you put on someone else's "hat," you view an issue from their perspective. How can this practice improve performance at work?

C Check your understanding. Go to page 58.

Step 2 Tell your story

A THINK In your online course, you thought about a time when someone made a decision that had a negative effect on you. Did the decision maker use perspective taking to find a compromise? How? If not, do you wish they had? Listen to the example.

B PAIRS Discuss your story.

C SHARE Tell your story to the class.

Step 3 Take away

A PAIRS Review your notes from the online module and complete the steps you should follow when using perspective taking. Use one word in each gap.

include	solutions	opinions	view	analyze	perspective

Steps in perspective taking

1 Clear your mind of your own ______________.

2 Get to know the people you disagree with and try to ______________ the issue from their ______________.

3 Take the perspectives of everyone involved to ______________ the most perspectives possible.

4 Take a 360-degree view of the issue: ______________ it from all the different points of view to find the best ______________.

B SHARE Check your answers with the class.

Step 4 Activate your knowledge

A THINK Imagine you are an employee in a small office. Look at these new programs your company is considering. Decide if you are for or against each of them and write down the reasons for your choices.

Proposed new office programs

1

"Bring your child to work" days

☐ For ☐ Against

Reasons: ______________________________

____

2

Wednesdays with no email and only face-to-face communication with colleagues

☐ For ☐ Against

Reasons: ______________________________

____

3

Monthly "volunteering on Saturday" program

☐ For ☐ Against

Reasons: ______________________________

____

4

Weekly "bring your pet to work" days

☐ For ☐ Against

Reasons: ______________________________

____

B GROUPS of 3–5 Read and listen to the conversation. Then role-play a company meeting where employees discuss the other proposed changes from A and together think of a compromise. Use perspective taking and what you know about your classmates to fully understand how people feel about each change.

A: I think "bring your child to work" days are a great idea. It would be a good chance to teach my kids about my job.
B: I agree. I think it would be a great experience for my kids, too.
C: I see your points, but I'm against it. I don't have kids, and I think having a lot of kids in the office would make it harder to get things done. I've got so much work to do!
A: That's an important point. I was thinking it would be interesting from the perspective of the kids, but I understand that it could be distracting.
B: How about we organize some activities for the kids in one of the big conference rooms? Then the kids will be kept busy with an activity and everyone who needs to can concentrate on their work.
C: I like that idea. Parents can show their kids around in the morning and tell them about their jobs, while those of us who don't have kids can focus on our work.
A: Great! And the kids could spend some time with each other if we have some games for them to play.
B: I agree. This sounds great.

C GROUPS of 3–5 When you need to make a decision as a group, it is useful to list all the arguments for and against the issue. This way, when you understand everyone's perspective, it is easier to find a solution that works for most people. Use a chart like the one below to write down all arguments for and against one of the office programs your group disagreed about in B.

"Bring your child to work" days

For	Against
1 *Teach children about work*	1 *Difficult to concentrate on work*
2 *Show the office to children and tell them about different jobs*	
3 *Children spend time together playing games*	

Step 5 Project

PAIRS In your online course, you interviewed two or three friends, family members, or colleagues about their experiences with perspective taking. Present the information you learned to your partner. Read the example.

I interviewed my sister, Lea, who was recently on a design team for a new product at her marketing firm. She had amazing ideas, but the team leader kept saying no because she wanted to keep things simple. At first, Lea thought the team leader just didn't like her ideas, but it later turned out the team had several other projects and were afraid of missing deadlines. They decided to talk to the design manager, who agreed to give some of their projects to other designers. This way the team could spend more time on the campaign. They used a lot of Lea's ideas, and they did great work!

Step 6 Talk!

PAIRS Perspective taking can be helpful in many situations. Discuss its importance in everyday life. Complete the questionnaire and compare your answers with your partner's. Use the questions below to help guide your conversation.

1. When you are telling the same story to different people, do you change any of the details depending on the knowledge and experience of your audience? ☐ Yes ☐ No
2. When someone asks you how to get to a nearby café, do you give directions differently if you know the person is just visiting your town? ☐ Yes ☐ No
3. When someone you just met asks you where you live, does your reply change depending on whether the person is from your region or a different part of the world? ☐ Yes ☐ No
4. Think of a problem you are dealing with at work or school right now. Can you easily describe the perspectives of 2–3 other people who you know are having the same problem? ☐ Yes ☐ No
5. Think of an issue that you have a strong opinion on. Can you easily provide arguments that are the opposite of your opinion? ☐ Yes ☐ No

- Do you do any of the things mentioned in the questionnaire? Why? Why not?
- If you answered no to any of the questions, can you think of reasons why it would be better to start doing those things? In what ways can they help us in everyday life?

Step 7 Going forward

A PAIRS In your online course, you reflected on which types of situations in your life you will handle differently after studying more about perspective taking. Discuss. Listen to the example.

B SHARE Present your ideas to the class.

VOCABULARY PRACTICE
Go to page 76.

I can explain the importance of perspective taking in the workplace. ☐

6

MODULE

Leadership

Leading a Group

DISCUSSION STRATEGIES

Go to page 68.

Step 1

Get started

A Refresh your memory! Watch the *What You'll Learn* video.

B Look at the photo. Do you enjoy being a leader? Why or why not?

C Check your understanding. Go to page 59.

Step 2 Tell your story

A THINK In your online course, you thought about a time that you were the leader of a group or a team at work, school, or in your personal life. Did you demonstrate any of the leadership skills you studied in your online module? Explain. Listen to the example.

B PAIRS Discuss your story.

C SHARE Tell your story to the class.

Step 3 Take away

A PAIRS Review your notes from the online module and match the phrases to complete the leadership skills.

Leadership skills

1	Inspiring others	a	and encouraging others to do so
2	Motivating others	b	with team members
3	Asking questions	c	with a vision
4	Not being afraid	d	to take risks
5	Sharing authority	e	and expecting others to do so
6	Taking responsibility	f	by appreciating their work and being a role model

B SHARE Check your answers with the class.

Step 4 Activate your knowledge

A PAIRS Read these leadership stories. Discuss which of the six leadership skills relate to each story. Explain why they were successful. Take notes.

1

I was the leader of a project team that worked remotely, that is, we all worked from home and rarely saw each other face to face. We met in person only once a month for a team meeting. After several months, I noticed progress was slowing down as if people had lost interest in the project. I tried talking to the team to see how we could work better together. I learned that most people needed more in-person meetings to keep them motivated, so I decided to increase them to once a week. The company didn't like the idea at first, but I promised my team's results would improve—and they did!

2

In my first leadership role, I was placed in charge of a large design team. Back then, I thought that being a leader meant making all the decisions and telling everyone what to do and what they did wrong. Well, after a few months, the team wasn't on schedule and people didn't seem happy, and I realized it was my fault. That's when I decided to invite the team to take part in a project planning and decision-making meeting. I wanted to make them feel that their work was important, and I thanked them for their ideas. Things started to improve quickly after that.

___

___

___

3

One of the insurance sales teams in my company was not performing well, so my managers asked me to help them identify problems that were affecting sales. One problem was the old, unclear vision statement, "Be the best in the business." It applied to any business and didn't really inspire anyone. I held a team meeting to discuss the new ideas I had, and I let the team vote for the one they liked best, which was, "Selling customers the insurance they need with the fastest, friendliest service anywhere." Then we discussed exactly what it meant so that everyone understood how to put it into action. The next quarter, sales were up more than 15%!

___

___

___

B SHARE **What did you learn about being a leader from the stories you read? Share your ideas with another pair.**

C SHARE **Present your ideas to the class.**

Step 5 Project

GROUPS of 3–4 In your online course, you interviewed someone in a leadership role in a company, university, sports team, or other organization. Describe the person you interviewed and present the information you learned. Read the example.

I interviewed a friend of mine who's the manager of a small financial services office. When it comes to taking responsibility, he said he is always available to answer questions and help deal with problems. At the same time, the employees take responsibility for their own clients' accounts to help the clients reach their financial goals. This way, the company offers the highest level of customer service.

Step 6 Talk!

PAIRS Read the quotations. Choose the one you think is the best advice and explain why.

The ability to learn is the most important quality a leader can have.

—Padmasree Warrior (b. 1961)
Indian-American businesswoman and technology manager

It's much, much better to talk to one another than about one another.

—Angela Merkel (b. 1954)
Chancellor of Germany from 2005 to 2021

Treat people you do business with as if they were a part of your family.

—Konosuke Matsushita (1894–1989)
Japanese businessman who founded Panasonic

Fight for the things that you care about, but do it in a way that will lead others to join you.

—Ruth Bader Ginsburg (1933–2020)
U.S. lawyer and justice of the Supreme Court of the United States

Step 7 Going forward

A PAIRS In your online course, you reflected on which types of situations that involve leadership you will handle differently after studying more about leadership skills. Discuss. Listen to the example.

B SHARE Present your ideas to the class.

VOCABULARY PRACTICE Go to page 77.

I can explain the importance of leadership skills and describe specific leadership strategies. ☐

Self-Management

Time Logs

DISCUSSION STRATEGIES

Go to page 68.

Step 1 Get started

A Refresh your memory! Watch the *What You'll Learn* video.

B Look at the photo. What do you think is happening? What may be the reason?

C Check your understanding. Go to page 60.

Step 2 Tell your story

A THINK In your online course, you thought about a time that you needed to finish a difficult task in a short time. Did you meet the deadline? What did you do? Listen to the example.

B PAIRS Discuss your story.

C SHARE Tell your story to the class.

Step 3 Take away

PAIRS Make a list of 5–8 time management tips that you think are most useful. Use ideas from the course and any others you know.

Time management tips

- ☐ *Reduce interruptions—let others know when you're busy, close your office door, turn off notifications in your phone.*
- ☐
- ☐
- ☐

Step 4 Activate your knowledge

A PAIRS Read the scenarios. Look at each person's time log to see how much time they planned to spend on their tasks and how long they actually take. Top priority tasks are labeled "TP." Then complete the last column to identify the time sponges.

1

Farzad is an IT technician. The company he works for is growing fast and he has to make sure staff members have all the tools they need to do their work. He is the only IT technician in the company and does not have enough time for his top priority tasks.

Work activity (hours per week)	Planned time	Actual time spent	Difference
Maintaining and testing network (TP)	15	9	
Responding to staff's software issues (TP)	11	8	
Helping staff with hardware issues	2	2	
Helping staff with account issues	2	4	
Purchasing hardware in stores	2	4	
Responding to general employee emails	4	7	
Answering employee phone calls	3	3	
Staff meetings	1	3	

2

Marta is the manager of a city tourist office. She has two full-time employees and several part-time tour guides. They are all getting ready for the busy season. Marta has received a special grant to plan and promote new tours and the deadline is next month.

Work activity (hours per week)	Planned time	Actual time spent	Difference
Planning new city tours (TP)	14	7	
Designing new brochures (TP)	11	6	
Training new guides	3	6	
Daily staff meetings	3	5	
Taking photos for website and brochures	2	5	
Ordering items for the gift shop	1	1	
Scheduling guided tours by phone	2	5	
Talking with customers	2	3	

B PAIRS **Choose the suggestions below that could help Farzad and Marta manage their time better. Can you think of any other solutions? Take notes.**

Solutions	Farzad	Marta
Use the "twice-a-day" and "one touch" rules for emails.	☐	☐
Have an employee talk with customers and call him or her only when it is necessary.	☐	☐
Schedule less time for top priority projects.	☐	☐
Make sure each meeting has a clear agenda.	☐	☐
Write tips for staff on how to remember and safely store logins and passwords.	☐	☐
Hire a local guide to help plan new tours.	☐	☐
Order hardware online instead of buying it in stores.	☐	☐
Say "no" to some staff meetings and ask a co-worker to take notes.	☐	☐
Talk to people in person whenever possible.	☐	☐
Buy photos online.	☐	☐
Use a digital calendar to schedule guided tours.	☐	☐
Use the "parking lot" method during meetings.	☐	☐
	☐	☐
	☐	☐

C SHARE **Compare your time-management suggestions for Farzad and Marta with another pair's. Take notes as you listen and give each other feedback.**

Step 5 Project

GROUPS of 3–5 In your online course, you researched 8–10 common time-management mistakes. Share your list of ideas with the group and explain why you thought they would be useful for your classmates to hear about. Read the example.

The first time-management mistake on my list is trying to do everything too perfectly. I think a lot of people forget you can't always be perfect at everything, and sometimes you really shouldn't! Those people lose a lot of time focusing on every small detail instead of what's really important. If this happens to you, you could ask your manager for feedback to learn what they think is most important.

Step 6 Talk!

PAIRS Many people have their own ways of managing time. Read about these time-management personality types. Discuss them using the questions below.

Action Hero
To the Action Hero, everything seems like an emergency. If something must be done, this person starts doing it immediately.

Dreamer
Dreamers always think they can complete a task quickly, no matter how big or difficult it is. Of course, they always end up behind schedule.

Multitasker
The Multitasker tries to do many things at once. You might find this person writing a report and talking on the phone while keeping an eye on downloading files.

Soldier
The Soldier follows the path forward no matter what. This person works very hard, is very independent, and always follows the plan.

"Yes" Person
The "Yes" Person hasn't learned to say "no." This person immediately agrees to do any task or favor when asked.

Perfectionist
The Perfectionist is unhappy with even the slightest mistake. This person stresses out when given more work than they can do perfectly.

- Do you recognize any of these time-management personality types in yourself? What do you think makes you behave this way?
- Which personality types have you worked with? Which do you find easy and which do you find difficult to work with?

Step 7 Going forward

A PAIRS In your online course, you reflected on which types of situations in life you will handle differently after studying more self-management skills. Discuss. Listen to the example.

B SHARE Present your ideas to the class.

VOCABULARY PRACTICE
Go to page 78.

I can describe specific strategies for improving my time management skills. ☐

8 MODULE

Wellness

Balancing Your Wellness Dimensions

DISCUSSION STRATEGIES

Go to page 68.

Step 1 Get started

A Refresh your memory! Watch the *What You'll Learn* video.

B Look at the photo. Which dimensions of wellness does this activity support?

C Check your understanding. Go to page 61.

Step 2 Tell your story

A THINK In your online course, you thought about a time you needed or wanted to improve your wellness and what you did. Listen to the example.

B PAIRS Discuss your story.

C SHARE Tell your story to the class.

Step 3 Activate your knowledge

A PAIRS Read these social media posts about jobs. Discuss which of the people's dimensions of wellness are strong, and which need strengthening. Explain why and take notes.

1

Diane Johansen

I've been working in the City Department of Youth Services for several months now, and I really enjoy helping young people find their way in life. It's such important work. I enjoy meeting them and their families, I only wish I didn't have so many cases! To be honest, I think it's too much work for one person, and I'm having trouble sleeping some nights. I could take some time off, but I'm uncomfortable doing that because I feel I should always be there for my clients. Sometimes I need to work weekends, too, so I had to quit my Saturday creative writing group, which is too bad. I really enjoyed going there and meeting other writers. On the positive side, I've become good friends with several members of the staff, and we meet for coffee just before work. I really should start the day with breakfast, though, because I often skip meals later in the day. There's just so much going on at work! On most days I snack a lot, but at least I make time to work out.

72 Likes 12 Comments

+ ______________________

– ______________________

2

Davon Thomas

After college, I got a job in another city at a big insurance company. I've been working there for a year now. The truth is I mostly fill out forms all day, which isn't interesting, but the salary is good. It's not very stressful, and I'm pretty happy here. I'm certainly not planning on quitting, but at the same time, I feel that my job isn't really helping the world very much. I would love to do something that made me feel like I was making the world a better place. After work, I usually go straight to the gym to work out and then go home since I still don't have many friends in this town. I'd like to make friends with some of my colleagues, but they don't go out after work and we seem to be interested in different things. I'd have to say I'm a little lonely sometimes. That's why I'm really glad I bought an e-reader. I download and read a lot of books on environmental science. It's something I'm interested in.

86 Likes 9 Comments

+ ______________________

– ______________________

B PAIRS Look at the photos. Discuss the activities that might help Diane and Davon strengthen their wellness dimensions.

C SHARE Present your ideas to the class.

Step 4 Take away

A GROUPS of 3–5 Discuss how strengthening the different dimensions of wellness can affect employability. Complete the diagram with your group's suggestions for each of the wellness dimensions.

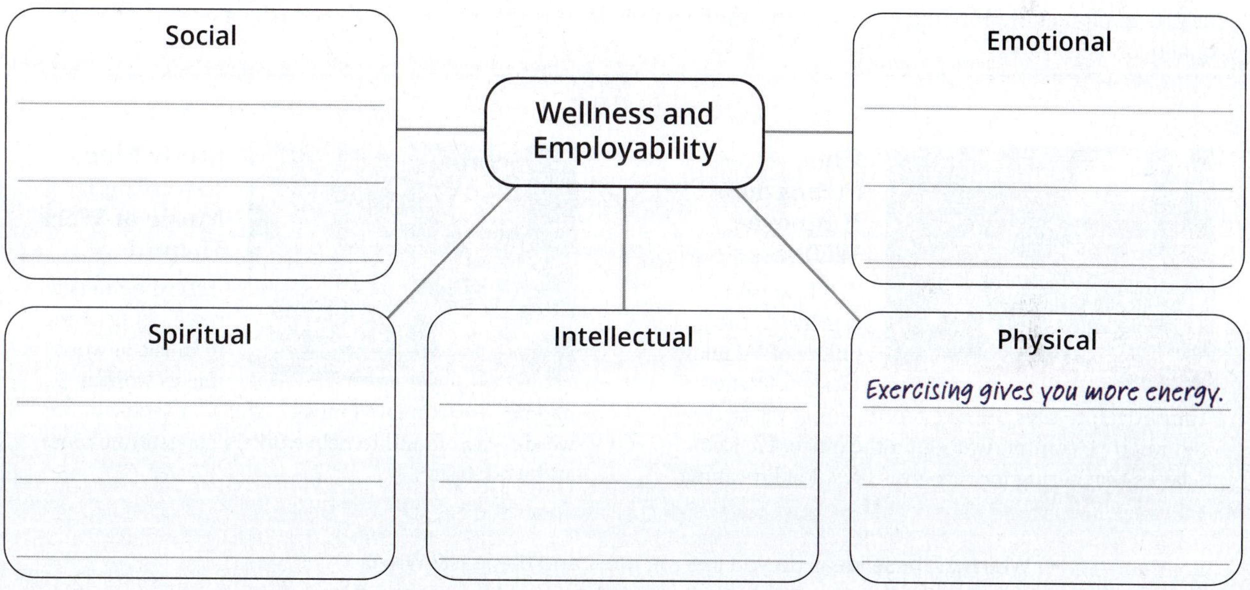

B SHARE Compare your ideas with another group's. What can you add to your list?

Step 5 Project

PAIRS In your online course, you created a list of 5–8 tips for how to improve one of the five dimensions of wellness presented in this module (physical, intellectual, spiritual, social, or emotional). Share those tips with your partner and discuss which seem the most useful. Read the example.

I researched tips for physical wellness, especially in the workplace. I read about an interesting study which showed that people who eat alone often have bigger and less healthy meals. So instead of eating at your desk, have lunch with your co-workers. It's better for your health and you can improve your social wellness at work at the same time!

Step 6 Talk!

PAIRS Read about these unusual wellness ideas in the workplace. Then discuss. Use the questions below to help guide your conversation.

Plants at Work Improve Employee Health

A university study showed that employees in offices with plants use fewer sick days. It was also found that plants not only improved the air quality but also helped employees improve the quality of their work.

Company Has Giant Slide between Floors

All the employees at Hamstead Computing are talking about their new giant slide. They say it's faster than the elevator, reduces stress on busy days, and makes them feel like kids again.

Game Room Brings Employees Together

Stress disappears when workers at Larkmont Systems enter their company game room and they focus instead on video, table, and board games. And it's also about making new friends.

Cats Strengthen Employee Wellness

Ten beautiful cats live in the offices of Edgeford Design. Owner Tom Edgeford says the cats reduce employee stress and improve communication in the office. He also believes that caring for cats gives life added meaning.

Study Finds Listening to Music at Work Helpful

According to new research, listening to music at work makes workers happier. Instrumental music—that is, music without words—was found to help workers concentrate more and work faster.

- Which of these ideas do you like the most and the least? Why?
- How do these ideas support different dimensions of wellness?
- What are other ways workplaces can support employee wellness?

Step 7 Going forward

A PAIRS In your online course, you reflected on how you would support your wellness differently after studying more about the different dimensions. Discuss. Listen to the example.

B SHARE Present your ideas to the class.

VOCABULARY PRACTICE Go to page 79.

I can describe the dimensions of wellness and strategies for improving wellness. ☐

9

MODULE

Social Responsibility

Diversity and Inclusion

DISCUSSION STRATEGIES

Go to page 68.

Step 1

Get started

A Refresh your memory! Watch the *What You'll Learn* video.

B Look at the photo. Along with hiring a diverse team, companies need to create an environment where everyone is supported. What are some ways that companies can promote an inclusive work culture?

C Check your understanding. Go to page 62.

Step 2 Tell your story

A THINK In your online course, you thought about a time when you were a new member of a group. Did you feel included or excluded? What made you feel this way? Listen to the example.

B PAIRS Discuss your story.

C SHARE Tell your story to the class.

Step 3 Activate your knowledge

A THINK Read the scenarios about problems that companies are having with building inclusive work environments. Using tips from your online module and your own ideas, write possible solutions to the problems.

1

April is a supervisor at a growing startup. She recently hired ten interns for a new summer internship program. She was really excited about the new ideas and enthusiasm they would bring to the team. The interns, however, are not contributing new or exciting ideas. They seem to be following the ideas of the employees who have been with the company for several years. In meetings, the interns are very quiet and agree with the ideas that have been shared already instead of giving their own ideas. In addition, during breaks, the employees and interns never talk with each other and April worries that this has created an unfriendly work environment.

____

____

____

____

2

Influenced Media, a social media advertising company, has customers across the globe. They have recently grown their sales team to increase their diversity. This has resulted in about 70% of the staff working in the office, and 30% working remotely and attending meetings virtually. The people working in person have strong relationships with each other but not with the remote employees, and they often seem to forget that the remote employees are there. Meetings usually end before remote employees have had a chance to speak. Another problem is that sometimes meetings are scheduled at times when remote employees are not able to attend due to time differences or are on days that are national holidays in their countries.

____

____

____

____

3

A big company with offices in six countries recently announced that one of their main goals for the year is to improve the diversity and inclusion (D&I) within their teams. They told all the managers to make this a top priority. The managers are all working on D&I, but everyone is doing something different and there has not been much progress. They all have different ideas and ways to increase diversity and how to make the workplace more inclusive.

B PAIRS Discuss your solutions with a partner. Take notes.

C SHARE Choose a scenario that you would like to present to the class. Review your notes and briefly describe your solutions to solving the problem.

Step 4 Take away

A PAIRS If your company does not have a D&I plan, there are still ways to make teams more inclusive. Create a checklist of how individuals can contribute to the inclusivity of a workplace or team. Use your notes from the online module and examples from Step 3.

How I can contribute to team inclusivity

- ☐ *I can make sure not to interrupt other co-workers when they're sharing ideas.*
- ☐
- ☐
- ☐

B SHARE Compare your list with another pair's. What can you add to your list?

Step 5 Project

PAIRS In your online course, you researched the D&I policies of two companies. Then you took notes on the different ways to increase diversity and inclusion in the workplace that were not covered in your online module. Share and compare your findings with a partner. Read the example.

I researched the D&I policies of two companies I'm interested in working for. One has a very big focus on making their office space fully accessible for differently abled people. As a person who uses a wheelchair, I was excited to see that I would have access to every part of the office. Another company I looked at is based in a different country, and every employee works remotely. At first, I wondered how they could create an inclusive environment when no one meets in person, but I found that they have a lot of activities and programs to help co-workers get to know one another. There are book clubs, trivia games, yoga classes, and a ton of other online activities that help people find things they have in common and develop friendships.

Step 6 Talk!

GROUPS of 3–5 One way to build an inclusive environment is to encourage team members to get to know each other as individuals. This helps people find out what they have in common and can improve working relationships. Read the different ideas for icebreaker activities. If you were the D&I officer and you wanted to conduct an icebreaker activity, which of these would you choose? Why? Is there another one you would rather do?

Travel map
One way to get to know each other is to find out about where people are from, where they have traveled, or where they want to go! Draw a star on the map in the place you were born. Then, draw a circle on a spot that you have visited or would like to visit. Share your two spots with your group.

Two truths and a lie
Spend up to five minutes thinking of three interesting facts about yourself. Two of these facts are true and one is a lie. Then, take turns sharing your three facts with the group. When a team member is sharing their three facts, the group guesses which is the lie.

"Get to know each other" questions
Discuss the questions below as a group. For more discussion questions, do an internet search for "Fun discussion questions".

- What is a food that everyone you know seems to love but you don't like?
- If you could only listen to one song for the rest of your life, which song would you choose and why?
- What is a movie that scared you as a kid?
- If you were trapped on a desert island, what are the three things you would want to have with you?

Step 7 Going forward

A PAIRS In your online course, you reflected on the types of situations in your life you will handle differently now that you have studied about diversity and inclusion. Discuss. Listen to the example.

B SHARE Present your ideas to the class.

VOCABULARY PRACTICE
Go to page 80.

I can explain the importance of diversity and inclusion in the workplace. ☐

10 MODULE

Branding

Building Your Personal Brand

DISCUSSION STRATEGIES
Go to page 68.

Step 1 Get started

A Refresh your memory! Watch the *What You'll Learn* video.

B Look at the photo. What does each outfit say about the person's brand? What are some other ways people can define their personal brand?

C Check your understanding. Go to page 63.

Step 2 Tell your story

A THINK In your online course, you thought about a time you used your online presence to strengthen your personal brand. Listen to the example.

B PAIRS Discuss your story.

C SHARE Tell your story to the class.

Step 3 Activate your knowledge

A PAIRS Read about these two famous people and look at their personal brand profiles. How well do their brand statements match their profiles? Discuss.

Dorothy Vaughan (1910–2008) was a U.S. mathematician and computer programmer. She completed her studies with a B.A. degree and worked as a math teacher to help support her family. In 1943 she joined NASA (National Aeronautics and Space Administration). She first worked with a group of African-American women called the "human computers" because they did complex mathematical calculations used for flight research within the space program. In 1949 she became the first African-American supervisor and one of a few female managers at NASA. Before NASA started using computers, she taught herself and her co-workers programming to help them prepare for the change. She supported all of her female co-workers, and helped to improve their working conditions and fight for promotions and pay raises.

Brand profile

Values: education, hard work, responsibility, teamwork, equality, family

Key activities: teaching at school, working as a mathematician for NASA, supervising a group of mathematicians, learning and teaching computer programming

Positive branding adjectives: intelligent, dedicated, passionate, motivated, caring

Skills: leadership, analytical skills, research skills, computer programming languages

Suggested brand statement: "I'm a dedicated mathematician and manager who believes that through education and working hard every day as a team we can make the world a better place for everyone."

Gabriel García Márquez (1927–2014) was one of the greatest writers of the twentieth century. He was the first Colombian to win a Nobel Prize for Literature (1982). He was raised by his grandparents. They told him stories about his hometown and his family that later made him want to write about them. He studied law and worked as a journalist in Colombia and abroad before becoming a famous writer. He was the author of many novels and short stories. One of his most famous novels is *One Hundred Years of Solitude*. It tells the story about a family in a small town of Macondo and at the same time brings to light the history of Latin America. It also represents a new style known as magical realism, which combines facts and true stories with elements of magic and dreams.

Brand profile

Values: imagination, knowledge, truth, culture, family

Key activities: studied law, working as a journalist, writing novels and short stories

Positive branding adjectives: creative, intelligent, ambitious, clever

Skills: communication skills, storytelling, research skills, critical thinking

Suggested brand statement: "I'm a creative writer who believes in the power of literature to help us better understand our everyday reality, ourselves, and the world."

B THINK Choose a famous person that your classmates might want to know more about. Complete their brand profile using what you know and what you can find online. Write their brand statement based on the information you have.

Brand profile

Name: ________________________________

Values: ________________________________

Key activities: ________________________________

____

Positive branding adjectives: ________________________________

____

Skills: ________________________________

____

Suggested brand statement: ________________________________

____

____

C PAIRS Tell your partner about the person you chose. Explain how their brand profile helps build their brand identity. Share the brand statement. Take notes while listening. If you can improve the brand statement, offer suggestions.

Step 4 Take away

A PAIRS Review your notes from the online module and complete the statements about personal branding. Use one word in each gap.

enhance Social media describe expertise Building résumé combination effective honest

- Your personal brand is how others see you and ________ you.
- It's a ________ of value, skills, personality, passion, and vision.
- ________ and controlling your personal brand is crucial to career success.
- Remember to be ________ when you are creating your brand.
- A personal brand needs to be authentic to be ________.
- Identify the skills and ________ that make you stand out from the crowd.
- You need to make sure your personal brand shines through on your ________.
- ________ is an important way of building your personal brand.
- You can ________ your online presence by sharing articles with colleagues.

B SHARE Check your answers with the class.

Step 5 Project

PAIRS In your online course, you created or developed your personal brand and wrote a personal branding statement for yourself. Present your brand and explain how your brand statement makes you stand out from the crowd. Read the example.

I would like to get a new job teaching at a private language school. So, this is how I wrote my personal branding statement. First, I thought about some of my positive branding adjectives: intelligent, motivated, creative, caring. Then I thought about my key activities: I love teaching young people, I'm a good communicator, and I prepare excellent lessons. Then I put these together to create my brand: "I'm an intelligent and motivated teacher with creative ideas, who cares deeply about my students, and has five years of teaching experience." I hope this makes me stand out and explains who I am.

Step 6 Talk!

GROUPS of 3–5 Discuss the importance of your online presence and personal branding. Use the facts and questions to help guide your conversation.

- Do you think it is possible to keep your private and professional lives separate on social media? Why? Why not?
- How can you know if your brand presents the right message about yourself?
- Can you build a successful career without being active online? Are there any professions that do not require it?

The average social media user has **8.4** different accounts.

65% of all internet users trust an online search the most as a source of information about people and companies.

90% of hiring managers said they checked likely candidates online.

45% of all internet users use social media for business.

Only **20%** of all job openings are posted online.

Step 7 Going forward

A PAIRS In your online course, you reflected on which types of situations in your life you will handle differently after studying more about personal branding. Discuss. Listen to the example.

B SHARE Present your ideas to the class.

VOCABULARY PRACTICE
Go to page 81.

I can explain the importance of personal branding and describe strategies for building my brand. ☐

11 MODULE

Job Search

How to Build a Network

DISCUSSION STRATEGIES

Go to page 68.

Step 1 Get started

A Refresh your memory! Watch the *What You'll Learn* video.

B Look at the photo. Do you feel more comfortable networking in person or online? Why?

C Check your understanding. Go to page 64.

Step 2 Tell your story

A THINK In your online course, you thought about a time your online contacts helped you make progress in your personal or professional life. Did you ask your network for support, or did your contacts offer help themselves? Listen to the example.

B PAIRS Discuss your story.

C SHARE Tell your story to the class.

Step 3 Activate your knowledge

A THINK You are going to participate in a networking activity with your classmates. Write a 30-second description of yourself to share when you meet someone for the first time. Include the most important points about yourself and your career goals. Read the example.

I'm Melissa Fuentes. I recently graduated with a bachelor's degree in business management. I got some excellent real-world experience as an intern at a top financial firm over the last four months. I'm passionate about project management and I'm looking for new challenges. I hope to apply what I've learned in a junior project management position in the financial field.

My name is...

B GROUPS of 3–5 Role-play a networking event in your classroom. Learn as much as you can about each person you network with. Use these directions as a guide. Take notes.

1 Greet each other and give a short description of yourselves that you prepared in 3A. Try to remember 2–3 main points from the other person's introduction.

2 Then ask one or two questions about the person focusing on the main points from their introduction, for example:

Experience and position:
- What is your current/dream job?
- What exactly do/did you do at…?
- What skills do you have that make you stand out?
- How did your education prepare you for your (future) job?
- What do/did you enjoy the most and the least about your job/internship?

Industry:
- Why do you want to work in this industry?
- What are some specific jobs available in this field?
- What education/experience would you need to work in this field?
- What skills should someone new to the field develop to be successful in the future?

Organization:
- What kind of company would you like to work for?
- What does your company do?
- What is/was the company culture like at…?
- What are the most important qualities that your company is looking for in new employees?

Career path:
- What made you choose this career?
- What do you do to develop professionally?
- How did you get started in your job?
- Do you have any advice for someone who wants a similar career?

3 Find out the best way to keep in touch and get the person's contact information.

4 Finish by thanking the person and promising to follow up.

C SHARE Was there anything about networking that you found difficult? Would you do anything differently next time? Discuss what you learned that you could use in different networking situations in the future.

Step 4 Take away

A PAIRS Effective networking is not just about making connections. You need to continue connecting with your contacts over time to build a strong and supportive network. Make a list of 5–8 ways to strengthen relationships within your network. Use ideas from the course and any others you know.

How to strengthen your network

- ☐ *Share articles or posts that are related to your contacts' profession or interests.*
- ☐
- ☐
- ☐

B SHARE Compare your list with another pair's. What can you add to your list?

Step 5 Project

PAIRS In your online course, you researched professional networking sites that are new to you. Share your research with your partner. Explain why you think the sites could be useful. Read the example.

One of the sites I researched is AngelList. It's mainly for people who want to work for a young, small company that is doing something innovative. You create your profile and upload your résumé like on other sites, but you can write to the people in the company directly, so it's more personal. It also has a great "matching" feature—you can choose the companies you're interested in, and they will contact you when they might have a job for you.

Step 6 Talk!

GROUPS of 3–5 Networking events are a great way of making connections. Read about different ideas for networking events and activities. Then discuss the questions.

Networking Ideas to Help People Connect

Mobile event app
Mobile apps allow participants to chat with people they want to network with and plan meetups even before the event starts. During the event, users can take part in different activities, leave questions for experts to answer, find other participants with similar interests, and share contact information by simply pressing a button.

Speed networking
A quick and easy way to make new connections is speed networking. Everyone has 5 minutes to talk to someone they have never met. They tell each other something about themselves and ask each other follow-up questions. When the time is up, everyone finds someone else to talk to. There are often competitions with prizes.

Virtual games and activities
People will create stronger networks if they have fun together or get a chance to work as a team. Popular fun activities include online quizzes, photo contests on social media, virtual dinner parties, and karaoke or yoga sessions.

- Which of these ideas seem the most interesting to you? Why?
- Have you ever attended an event that used one or more of these ideas?
- In what ways can these ideas make networking more effective or enjoyable?
- Do you have any other ideas for networking activities that have not been discussed?

Step 7 Going forward

A PAIRS In your online course, you reflected on which types of situations in your life you will handle differently after studying more about networking skills. Discuss. Listen to the example.

B SHARE Present your ideas to the class.

VOCABULARY PRACTICE
Go to page 82.

I can explain the importance of networking and describe strategies for building my network. ☐

12 MODULE

Interviewing

Preparing for an Interview

DISCUSSION STRATEGIES

Go to page 68.

Step 1 Get started

A Refresh your memory! Watch the *What You'll Learn* video.

B Look at the photo. What are some of the most important things to do to prepare for a job interview?

C Check your understanding. Go to page 65.

Step 2 Tell your story

A THINK In your online course, you thought about a time you went to a job or internship interview. Were you well prepared? How did it go? Listen to the example.

B PAIRS Discuss your story.

C SHARE Tell your story to the class.

Step 3 Activate your knowledge

A THINK Listen to two candidates answering some common interview questions. Analyze their answers. What did they do correctly or incorrectly? Take notes.

Interview 1

✔ ______________________
____
____

✘ ______________________
____
____

Interview 2

✔ ______________________
____
____

✘ ______________________
____
____

B PAIRS Discuss what you think each person did well and what he or she could have done differently. Add any new ideas to your list.

C PAIRS You are going to role-play a job interview. Student A, you will answer the first set of questions. Student B, you will answer the questions in the second set. Prepare your answers. Take notes.

Interview questions

A

1 Describe a situation that required you to use leadership skills in life or at work.
____

2 What is your main weakness?
____

3 Tell me about a conflict you had with someone at school or at work and how you handled it.
____

4 Think about a time you wanted to make a good impression on others in life or at work. What did you do?
____

B

1 Tell me about a time you made a mistake in life or at work. What did you learn from it?

____

2 Think about a time you had a very heavy workload. How did you deal with it?

____

3 Tell me about a time you collaborated successfully with others.

____

4 Where do you see yourself in five years?

____

D PAIRS Take turns asking each other the interview questions. Remember to make a good impression on the interviewer. Take notes in the feedback form below while listening to your partner's answers. Then give each other feedback.

Interview feedback form

Candidate name: ________________________

The candidate made sure to:

- ☐ sound friendly and confident.
- ☐ make eye contact.
- ☐ speak clearly.
- ☐ provide only relevant information.

Notes: ____

E SHARE What did you learn from the role play both as the job candidate and the interviewer? Share your ideas with the class.

Step 4 Take away

A GROUPS of 3–5 Use your notes from Step 3 and any other ideas you have to create a list of interview dos and don'ts.

Interview dos	Interview don'ts
• *Prepare answers to common interview questions.*	• *Don't talk about unrelated subjects during the interview.*
• ________________	• ________________
• ________________	• ________________
• ________________	• ________________

B SHARE Compare your list with another group's. What can you add to your list?

Step 5 Project

A THINK In your online course, you researched five additional common interview questions and recommendations on how to answer them. Read the example.

Question: *What's your dream job?*

Tips I found: *Don't just talk about the job, remember to highlight some of your key skills and qualifications that will show you are a good candidate for this position.*

My answer: *My dream job is working in web development. I have strong creative and artistic abilities and working in web development would allow me to develop these skills while also learning new technical skills. This way, I could help the company be more competitive in the market.*

B PAIRS Have your partner ask you the questions and then explain why you answered them the way you did.

Step 6 Talk!

GROUPS of 3–5 Success in a job interview depends on many factors. Read these common job interview mistakes. How serious are they? Rank them from most to least serious.

Six interview mistakes that can prevent you from getting hired:

____ Not shaking hands properly.

____ Not telling the truth on your résumé.

____ Using an email address that is not professional.

____ Not making appropriate eye contact.

____ Knowing too little about the company.

____ Not showing enough confidence, using the wrong tone, or not smiling.

Step 7 Going forward

A PAIRS In your online course, you reflected on how you will handle job interviews differently after studying more about interview skills. Discuss. Listen to the example.

B SHARE Present your ideas to the class.

VOCABULARY PRACTICE
Go to page 83.

I can describe specific strategies for improving my interview skills. ☐

CHECK YOUR UNDERSTANDING

Check your understanding 1

REFRESH YOUR MEMORY!
Review the Online Course material in your Resources.

Choose the best answers. More than one answer may be correct in some items.

1 Which are examples of weak interpersonal communication skills when you are trying to motivate colleagues to do a better job?

- **a** making demands
- **b** giving direct criticisms to individuals
- **c** making requests

2 Body language is important in creating the right impression. What is an example of negative body language that you should avoid?

- **a** making eye contact
- **b** smiling
- **c** crossing your arms

3 What can make a good impression in an email?

- **a** An email with a subject line that summarizes the topic.
- **b** An email that is short and focused on the topic.
- **c** An email that includes friendly jokes and emojis.

4 While giving instructions, you should ____.

- **a** pause and ask if there are any questions
- **b** make requests with "please" and "thank you"
- **c** be clear and repeat your demands

5 Which of the following is true about *taking* criticism?

- **a** It is okay to be defensive if a co-worker gives feedback using an impolite tone.
- **b** It is not necessary to listen to negative feedback at work.
- **c** It is important to listen to criticism with an open mind.

6 Daniel has a virtual meeting with a new client. He is worried about making a good first impression. Since he cannot use body language, how can he show that he is actively listening during the meeting? Check all that are true.

- **a** He can avoid asking questions.
- **b** He can ask for clarification, if needed.
- **c** He can repeat what is said to check understanding.

7 What is wrong with the interpersonal communication skills used in this business email?

Hey Team! I LOVED the presentation you gave yesterday ☺. BUT can you please leave time for questions next time?

- **a** inappropriate tone
- **b** unprofessional
- **c** incorrect spelling

8 A meeting is about to begin when you notice the door is still open. Which of these examples is the most polite way to ask a colleague to close the door?

- **a** Can someone close the door?
- **b** Would you please close the door? Thanks!
- **c** Close the door. Thanks!

9 A meeting with an important client did not go well because one of the team members was not prepared. Which of these examples is an appropriate way to give negative feedback?

- **a** Yesterday's meeting did not go well. Let's discuss how we can fix it.
- **b** Yesterday's meeting did not go well because of Raj.
- **c** Yesterday's meeting was a complete failure. How are you going to fix that?

Check your understanding 2

REFRESH YOUR MEMORY!
Review the Online Course material in your Resources.

Choose the best answers. More than one answer may be correct in some items.

1 **What communication skills should you use in difficult situations?**
- **a** Wait until you are calm to speak.
- **b** Convince others they are wrong.
- **c** Listen carefully to make sure you understand.

2 **What is the most polite way to respond to a colleague who is unhappy with your work?**
- **a** Tell them to give you suggestions on how to improve your work.
- **b** Ask them for suggestions on how to improve your work.
- **c** Give them reasons why your work does not need improvement.

3 **Why is it helpful to summarize your understanding of a problem to the customer?**
- **a** It clears up misunderstandings and shows you were listening.
- **b** It shows that you know how to deal with angry customers.
- **c** It shows the customer that you are serious about your job.

4 **What are some guidelines for dealing with customer problems?**
- **a** Do your best to fix the problem.
- **b** Follow up to make sure the problem is resolved.
- **c** Wait until angry customers are calm.

5 **What is the most respectful way to respond to the following complaint from a hotel guest?**
Our room has not been cleaned. The bed isn't made, and we were not given fresh towels. I thought this was a four-star hotel!
- **a** It's only 1:00 in the afternoon. Housekeeping will get to your room soon.
- **b** Please accept my sincere apology. We'll send housekeeping to your room right away.
- **c** We'll send someone to clean your room and bring fresh towels when we can.

6 **What communication mistake does Catherine make in the following conversation?**
Patrick: To improve sales, I think we should start marketing our products to teenagers.
Catherine: What? I totally disagree! Teenagers have completely different needs and interests. Why would they want to buy our products?
- **a** She uses language that is not respectful.
- **b** She summarizes her understanding of the problem.
- **c** She makes it clear that she has a better idea.

7 **What communication skills should Chris use to improve his response to the manager?**
Manager: Chris, do you have time for a quick meeting? I need to discuss a complaint with you.
Chris: Give me five minutes. I just need to finish writing this email first.
Manager: OK, I'll be waiting for you in the conference room.
Chris: Cool! See you in a few minutes.
- **a** He should ask the manager to resolve the complaint.
- **b** He should show more respect in his answers.
- **c** He should use less casual language.

8 **How should Chris respond to the following feedback from his manager? What should he say?**
Manager: An important client has been trying to reach you for a week, but you have not returned their calls or emails. I'm worried that we are going to lose this client.
- **a** "Tell them that I am sorry for the delay and will contact them as soon as possible."
- **b** "I'm sorry for not responding to their messages. You know, I've just been too busy."
- **c** "I'm really sorry for not getting back to them sooner. I'll contact them now."

Check your understanding 3

REFRESH YOUR MEMORY!
Review the Online Course material in your Resources.

Choose the best answer. More than one answer may be correct for some items.

1 What are some benefits of setting short- and long-term goals?
  a Setting long-term goals can help you achieve short-term goals.
  b Setting short-term goals can help you achieve long-term goals.
  c Setting short- and long-term goals can help you achieve success.

2 How can you make sure that your goals are SMART?
  a They need to include milestones that are relevant to people's lives.
  b They need to be measurable, relevant, and time-bound.
  c They need to be achievable and clearly defined.

3 What is a short-term goal?
  a It is a milestone for a long-term goal.
  b It is a final objective for a long-term goal.
  c It is a goal that can be easily accomplished.

4 Which of these examples is a short-term goal?
  a creating a website
  b finding a web-hosting service
  c getting a degree in graphic design

5 Which of these examples is a long-term goal?
  a writing an academic paper
  b becoming a university professor
  c registering for university courses

6 Read the long-term goal. Then choose the short-term goals that will help achieve it.
  The Global Business Program at our university has been losing money because the number of students has decreased. My goal is to increase the number of students by 15% within nine months.
  a I will assess students' needs and offer new courses to meet their needs.
  b I will market the program to new student populations.
  c I will increase tuition by 5% to compete with other first-rate schools.

7 Which SMART-goal criteria is included in this goal statement?
  Indira is tired of working at a bank. She wants to be a teacher. She plans to go back to school to get a teaching degree. She will take night classes and continue working at the bank.
  a Her goal is achievable.
  b Her goal is relevant.
  c Her goal is time-bound.

8 What is true about this goal statement?
  Andres wants to increase the size of his landscaping business. He plans to have at least 25 more clients by the end of spring.
  a The long-term goal is specific and measurable.
  b The short-term goal is relevant and time-bound.
  c The short- and long-term goals are achievable.

Check your understanding 4

REFRESH YOUR MEMORY!
Review the Online Course material in your Resources.

Choose the best answers. More than one answer may be correct in some items.

1 How can teams facilitate continuous communication?

a by changing team roles regularly

b by having regular meetings

c by scheduling projects regularly

2 What are some ways to structure a team effectively?

a choose the right team leader to make the decisions for the team

b assign tasks that match team members' strengths

c have the right number of team members

3 Which factors encourage effective collaboration?

a being reliable

b working with new people

c keeping good relationships with teammates

4 Who is responsible for a team's failure?

a the weakest team members

b the team leader

c all team members

5 Why is it important for teams to have a common goal?

a When there is a common goal, it helps teams work together to complete challenging tasks.

b When there is a common goal, team leaders can successfully make decisions for their team.

c When there is a common goal, teams can identify members who have weak skills.

6 A small company has been losing money for over a year. Each member of the leadership team has been trying to find the reason and develop a solution, but nothing seems to be helping. How can they improve the effectiveness of their team?

a They should assign one team member to work on the problem while others work on different tasks.

b They should meet to agree on the causes of the problem and work together to find solutions.

c They should hire new employees who are better able to identify and solve the problem.

7 Five co-workers are putting a report together. They have asked Amelia to be their team leader. She has assigned parts of the report to each person and suggested deadlines that everyone agreed on. She also scheduled a weekly standing meeting to check in on the team. What key characteristics of effective teamwork has Amelia used?

a She uses continuous communication to help the team stay on track.

b She uses collaboration effectively by assigning the right roles to each team member.

c She uses her role as team leader to tell the others exactly what they need to do to succeed.

8 Collaborating is very important when working in a group setting. Which examples illustrate successful collaboration?

a Daniel is careful to take credit for his team's success.

b Sheri attends team meetings and shares her ideas.

c Josh listens to his teammates' ideas.

9 Pierre's team created marketing materials for a product. Unfortunately, their work did not help increase product sales. Pierre's team blames him since he was the team leader. How can they improve their team's response to the problem?

a They should share the blame for the problem and come up with a solution together.

b They should remove Pierre from the team and choose a new team leader.

c They should convince Pierre to accept the blame and continue working on a solution.

10 Nora and Xuan own a successful flower shop. They each have similar skills, but they have different roles. Nora runs the shop and takes online orders, and Xuan puts together the flower arrangements. Nora leaves when the shop closes, but Xuan often has to work several more hours to finish her work. How can they improve the structure of their team?

a They should hire another employee to help with the workload.

b Nora should help Xuan finish the flower arrangements.

c They should have different roles so that they work more efficiently.

Check your understanding 5

REFRESH YOUR MEMORY!
Review the Online Course material in your Resources.

Choose the best answers. More than one answer may be correct in some items.

1 What is true about perspective taking?
- **a** It is most useful in workplaces where people have similar values.
- **b** It involves trying to understand other people's points of view.
- **c** It is a crucial skill for working with others successfully.

2 Perspective taking ____.
- **a** can lead to new ideas
- **b** can reveal people's strengths
- **c** can improve a team's creativity

3 Why is it important to clear your mind of your opinions when perspective taking?
- **a** It helps others understand your ideas.
- **b** It helps you strengthen your ideas.
- **c** It opens your mind to others' ideas.

4 What does it mean *to wear someone else's "hat"*?
- **a** It means that you agree with another person's point of view.
- **b** It means that you try to see an issue from another person's point of view.
- **c** It means that you make a compromise between different viewpoints.

5 When analyzing an issue, it is helpful to consider the most perspectives possible because ____.
- **a** it can help identify the best solution to a problem
- **b** it helps convince others that your viewpoint is the best
- **c** it can uncover ideas that you disagree with

6 The director of a community center decided to make changes to their youth program based on feedback received from some staff members. The director believed everyone would like the changes. Consider the mistakes the director made in perspective taking. What should she have done differently?
- **a** She should have made changes based only on her own background and experiences.
- **b** She should not have assumed she knew how everyone would feel about the changes.
- **c** She should have asked all staff members for their feedback before making changes.

7 Sophie likes to work on projects with colleagues who share her point of view. However, her manager thinks her projects could be more creative. How can Sophie use perspective taking to improve her work?
- **a** She should try to work with people who think differently from her.
- **b** She should make sure her work reflects her ideas.
- **c** She should consider more diverse points of view.

8 Juan surveyed his staff on how they could improve their customer service. Everyone had very different ideas. How can he use perspective taking to identify the best ideas?
- **a** He should identify the best ideas and share them with everyone.
- **b** He should take a 360-degree view of the issue by analyzing all views.
- **c** He should analyze the views from staff members that he trusts.

Check your understanding 6

REFRESH YOUR MEMORY!

Review the Online Course material in your Resources.

Choose the best answer. More than one answer may be correct in some items.

1 **Which are true about successful leaders?**

- **a** They encourage employees to participate in decision-making.
- **b** They usually use the same approach if it was successful before.
- **c** They always ask questions about how to improve things.

2 **How can leaders inspire the people in their organization?**

- **a** by helping employees to care about their work
- **b** by clarifying the organization's vision for the future
- **c** by encouraging employees to delegate tasks to others

3 **How can leaders motivate their team?**

- **a** by making a lot of money
- **b** by being a good role model
- **c** by acknowledging mistakes

4 **Effective leaders ask and encourage questions to ____.**

- **a** improve processes
- **b** recognize team members for their work
- **c** solve problems collaboratively

5 **Leaders are not afraid to take risks because ____.**

- **a** risky decisions usually have a positive result
- **b** risks can lead to innovative outcomes
- **c** failed risks can offer learning opportunities

6 **Why should a leader share authority with employees?**

- **a** It provides learning opportunities for the leader.
- **b** It gives employees a chance to earn more money.
- **c** It saves time and builds employees' skills.

7 **Why is taking responsibility for reaching goals an important leadership skill?**

- **a** It encourages trust and risk-taking.
- **b** It places all the blame on the leader.
- **c** It discourages employees from taking risks.

8 **We recently hired a new director. After two weeks, she started making changes to the structure of our organization. Many staff members are upset and do not understand why she is making these changes. Which leadership skill would help this situation?**

- **a** The director should motivate staff members by giving them a raise.
- **b** The director should share authority with the staff members.
- **c** The director should share her vision with the staff members.

9 **Aida works for a tech company that designs apps. She has some new innovative ideas she would like to share, but the program manager is not interested in hearing them. Which leadership skill would help this situation?**

- **a** The program manager should encourage questions and ideas.
- **b** The program manager should take responsibility for reaching goals.
- **c** The program manager should encourage risk-taking.

10 **Evan owns a woodworking business and has two employees. His employees are ready to take on more difficult tasks, but Evan is nervous about giving them more responsibility. Which leadership skills would help this situation?**

- **a** Evan should encourage questions from his employees.
- **b** Evan should share authority with his employees.
- **c** Evan should not be afraid to take a risk.

Check your understanding 7

REFRESH YOUR MEMORY! Review the Online Course material in your Resources.

Choose the best answer. More than one answer may be correct in some items.

1 What is a time log?

- **a** It is a tool used to keep meetings on track.
- **b** It is a tool used to identify how you spend your time.
- **c** It is a tool used to respond to email.

2 Which of the following is true about keeping a time log?

- **a** It improves productivity.
- **b** It provides meeting guidelines.
- **c** It helps you stay focused on your tasks.

3 Which are helpful ways to save time?

- **a** If an email takes more than five minutes, make a two-minute phone call instead.
- **b** Only do one thing with each email or voicemail: reply, forward, save, or delete it.
- **c** Check email and voicemail three days per week.

4 How can you keep meetings on track?

- **a** Topics that are not on the agenda should be "parked" for another meeting.
- **b** Topics could be decided on at the beginning of a meeting in order to create the agenda.
- **c** Meetings that do not have an agenda should be "parked" and rescheduled.

5 **Tanja manages a busy medical center. She is often behind schedule because she spends too much time meeting with staff and responding to emails throughout the day. How can Tanja save time?**

- **a** She should check email only twice a day at two set times.
- **b** She should take notes and record staff meetings.
- **c** She should say "no" to non-essential meetings.

6 **Miguel works for a design firm and has to attend many team meetings each day. He is also frequently interrupted by phone calls from clients. This does not leave him much time to design. Which suggestions might help him save time?**

- **a** He should let calls go through to voicemail and use the "one touch" rule.
- **b** He should review meeting recordings instead of attending non-essential meetings.
- **c** He should estimate less time for design projects so that he can attend essential meetings.

7 **Look at the time log. What can Shireen do about the work activities that take too much time? Choose the suggestion that might help.**

Work activity (hours/week)	Planned time	Actual time spent	Difference
Project 1 (top priority)	10	8	−2
Project 2 (top priority)	10	7	−3
Responding to emails	10	16	+6
Answering phone calls	4	3	−1
Office meetings	6	6	0

- **a** She should make more short phone calls instead of writing long emails.
- **b** She should give up one of her priority projects.
- **c** She should respond to emails as soon as she receives them.

8 **Hoa provides technology support for a large company. It is her job to make sure the network runs smoothly. She also helps co-workers with technology problems. Look at her time log. Then choose the suggestions that might help her manage her time better.**

Work activity (hours/week)	Planned time	Actual time spent	Difference
Researching new software	5	2	−3
Software maintenance	10	10	0
Responding to email	10	15	+5
Answering phone calls	8	7	−1
Staff meetings	3	4	+1
Tracking problems	4	2	−2

- **a** Hoa should let her calls go to voicemail and check them twice a day.
- **b** She should say "no" to more staff meetings and have a co-worker take notes for her.
- **c** She should only check emails twice, for example at the beginning and end of the day.

Check your understanding 8

REFRESH YOUR MEMORY!
Review the Online Course material in your Resources.

Choose the best answers. More than one answer may be correct for some items.

1 **You can strengthen your social wellness at work by ____.**
- **a** meditating once or twice a day
- **b** being a careful listener
- **c** offering encouragement and thanks

2 **How can you build emotional wellness?**
- **a** by controlling your workload
- **b** by avoiding negative feelings
- **c** by attending a stress-management workshop

3 **Spiritual wellness makes people feel ____.**
- **a** able to do more difficult tasks
- **b** a sense of fulfillment
- **c** talkative at work

4 **You can improve your physical wellness by ____.**
- **a** drinking a lot of coffee to give you energy
- **b** getting regular exercise that you enjoy
- **c** thinking about what you are eating

5 **How can you develop your intellectual wellness?**
- **a** by doing activities that inspire creativity
- **b** by tracking the number of steps you take each day
- **c** by taking a break from social media

6 **Tiana does not know her co-workers very well. This makes her feel uncomfortable during meetings. Think about the dimension of wellness that she needs to strengthen. Then choose the best advice.**
- **a** She should try to connect with her colleagues in relaxed and friendly ways.
- **b** She should politely say "no" to unnecessary meeting requests to reduce her stress.
- **c** She should meet with a counselor to share her feelings about work.

7 **Mahdi is feeling overwhelmed because his workload is too heavy. He is trying to meet a deadline, but his colleagues keep asking for his help with other projects. Think about the dimension of wellness that he needs to strengthen. Then choose the best advice.**
- **a** He should develop friendships with his colleagues and offer to help them.
- **b** He should not be afraid to say "no" to his colleagues' requests for assistance.
- **c** He should take care of himself physically by coming to work well rested.

8 **Lucas is good at his sales job and enjoys working with his colleagues. However, his job does not make him feel like he is making a difference in the world. Think about the dimension of wellness that he needs to strengthen. Then choose the best advice.**
- **a** He should strengthen his spiritual wellness by volunteering his time to help others.
- **b** He should strengthen his social wellness by having casual conversations with co-workers.
- **c** He should strengthen his intellectual wellness by traveling to a place he has not been before.

9 **John often falls asleep around midnight and wakes up at 5:30 to go to work. He drinks coffee throughout the day to help him stay awake and focused. Think about the dimension of wellness that he needs to strengthen. Then choose the best advice.**
- **a** John should exercise after work to help him stay awake until midnight.
- **b** John should reduce his stress level by practicing mindfulness or doing yoga.
- **c** John should replace unhealthy habits with healthier ones.

10 **Shay has been working in an administrative position for one year. She likes her job, but she still does not know how to use some computer software programs. This is creating some stress and challenges for her. Think about the dimension of wellness that she needs to strengthen. Then choose the best advice.**
- **a** She should strengthen her spiritual wellness by spending time in nature to clear her head.
- **b** She should strengthen her emotional wellness by taking some time off work.
- **c** She should strengthen her intellectual wellness by taking a course to improve her skills.

Check your understanding 9

REFRESH YOUR MEMORY! Review the Online Course material in your Resources.

Choose the best answers. More than one answer may be correct for some items.

1 What does it mean to have a diverse work environment?

- **a** It means that employees have traveled to different countries and met people from other cultures.
- **b** It means that employees have different ethnic backgrounds, cultures, gender identities, and experiences.
- **c** It means that managers have more work experience, skills, and qualifications than low-level employees.

2 An inclusive workplace means that ____.

- **a** diverse employees can work together without discrimination or intolerance
- **b** opportunities are given to the most diverse employees
- **c** employees are given the tools they need to fully participate

3 Companies should implement Diversity & Inclusion policies because ____.

- **a** they can be easily developed throughout an organization
- **b** they promote acceptance of people's differences
- **c** they create synergies that can bring out the best in staff

4 How do Diversity & Inclusion policies benefit companies?

- **a** They can attract new graduates who value diversity.
- **b** They can make companies more innovative.
- **c** They can identify diverse abilities among employees.

5 What are some ways that organizations and businesses can implement Diversity & Inclusion policies?

- **a** by making sure diversity exists in low-level positions first
- **b** by offering team building exercises to help people get to know each other
- **c** by making rules for employee behavior that promotes inclusivity

6 Employees can promote an inclusive environment during meetings by ____.

- **a** letting those who have worked there the longest speak the most often
- **b** letting valued team members have a chance to speak first
- **c** giving everyone an opportunity to share their ideas before ending a meeting

7 Company A has a strong mission statement that emphasizes diversity and inclusion, but they do not currently have formal D&I rules and are not sure where to begin. What should they do?

- **a** They should have diverse employees write D&I rules.
- **b** They should create an organizational inclusion plan.
- **c** They should create training programs to build inclusive teams.

8 A large technology company has been trying to increase diversity across the organization. They recently hired several women who are experienced software engineers for entry-level positions. How can the company go further to improve diversity?

- **a** They should hire experienced women for higher-level positions.
- **b** They should encourage experienced men to apply for low-level positions.
- **c** They should make sure diversity exists at all levels of the company.

9 Company B is trying hard to become a more diverse and inclusive company. One way they are doing this is by encouraging staff to work in multi-generational teams. How can this decision help improve the performance of the team?

- **a** It gives more experienced employees a way to show their skills and lead the team.
- **b** It offers younger employees an opportunity to learn from more experienced employees.
- **c** It gives employees of different ages a chance to find things in common and learn to work together.

10 Robert leads a monthly staff meeting that includes nine people. This week two new employees will join the meeting. What can Robert do to make sure the new employees feel valued?

- **a** He can give the new employees a chance to speak first.
- **b** He can stop people from interrupting the new employees.
- **c** He can ask new employees to take notes for everyone.

Check your understanding 10

REFRESH YOUR MEMORY!
Review the Online Course material in your Resources.

Choose the best answers. More than one answer may be correct for some items.

1 Which ones are part of personal branding?
- **a** appearance and reputation
- **b** values and personality
- **c** abilities and experience

2 A personal brand statement should ____.
- **a** highlight your education and experience
- **b** describe what makes you unique
- **c** include positive branding adjectives

3 Which ways can you include your personal brand on your résumé?
- **a** by stressing your expertise along with your experience and achievements
- **b** by including a personal photo and short biography about your life
- **c** by adding your personal branding statement below your contact information

4 Why is your online presence an important part of personal branding?
- **a** because it is an effective way to confirm and strengthen your brand
- **b** because it shows employers how much time you spend online
- **c** because information you share shows that your brand is authentic

5 Hee Seung is writing her personal brand statement. She has a lot of experience in the field of communications. Which of the following personal brand statements is the most effective?
- **a** I am a creative communications expert who is skillful at telling a company's unique story in a memorable way.
- **b** I have worked in communications for over a decade and enjoy working with clients to create their public image.
- **c** I am a communications professional with years of experience who is seeking a position as a public relations specialist.

6 Which keywords from this job announcement should Hee Seung try to include on her résumé?

Public Relations Specialist Wanted

We seek an experienced Public Relations Specialist to create, grow, and maintain our company's brand. Responsibilities include drafting press releases, building and maintaining relationships with media contacts, and analyzing media coverage. Our company is a great place to work!

- **a** press releases
- **b** relationships with media contacts
- **c** great place to work

7 André wants people to think that he cares about diversity and inclusion because he knows that companies value it. He shares articles about D&I with colleagues and friends regularly. However, he is not personally interested in this topic and often does not read the articles that he shares. How can André strengthen his personal branding and make it more authentic?
- **a** He should be honest and share what he cares about.
- **b** He should write a blog and post more about D&I.
- **c** He should share articles that he believes in.

8 A hiring manager at a construction company was deciding which candidates to interview for a project management position. The candidates had strong résumés. She noticed that one of them often complained about his last job and co-workers on Facebook. She decided not to offer him an interview. How can this job candidate strengthen his personal branding?
- **a** He can post both positive and negative comments about others on social media.
- **b** He can post about his professional accomplishments on social media.
- **c** He can delete negative posts about others from social media.

Check your understanding 11

REFRESH YOUR MEMORY!
Review the Online Course material in your Resources.

Choose the best answers. More than one answer may be correct for some items.

1 **What is networking?**
- **a** It is learning about how to improve your interpersonal communication skills.
- **b** It is meeting new people who have similar interests or do the same type of work.
- **c** It is taking professional development courses to expand your skills and knowledge.

2 **What are the benefits of having a network?**
- **a** People in your network can help you find a job.
- **b** People in your network can post everything about you.
- **c** People in your network can provide mutual support.

3 **What are some ways to build a professional network online?**
- **a** by connecting with someone new and asking them to help you as soon as possible
- **b** by joining groups in which members share information about certain types of jobs
- **c** by writing blogs related to your profession and posting them on social networking sites

4 **What are some ways to network in real life?**
- **a** talking with colleagues about your skills and interests
- **b** making new contacts at professional conferences
- **c** making small talk with new people that you meet

5 **You can strengthen your relationship with your network by ____.**
- **a** removing old contacts and regularly emailing new contacts
- **b** liking or commenting on other's social media posts
- **c** writing a recommendation for someone

6 **Annette has been a classroom teacher for many years and is experienced using technology in her lessons. She has been thinking about changing to a career in eLearning, but she is not sure which type of position she would like best. What can Annette do to network and learn more about the field of eLearning?**
- **a** She should attend a virtual career fair to talk to people who work in the field.
- **b** She should consider job shadowing for different positions within the field.
- **c** She should practice using new technologies with her students in the classroom.

7 **Robert is a sales representative for an insurance company. He needs to increase his sales by gaining new customers. How can Robert expand his network to reach new customers?**
- **a** He should join a social networking site like LinkedIn.
- **b** He should do an internship to meet more people.
- **c** He should network with people wherever he goes.

8 **Cleo has been applying for jobs in graphic design. He has a LinkedIn profile and has participated in some virtual networking events, but he has been having a hard time getting a job. What can Cleo do to enhance his reputation as a graphic designer?**
- **a** He should create an online portfolio of his work and share it on his social media profile.
- **b** He should research different companies online to identify the best graphic design positions.
- **c** He should connect with people online by sharing interesting articles or liking their posts.

Check your understanding 12

REFRESH YOUR MEMORY!
Review the Online Course material in your Resources.

Choose the best answers. More than one answer may be correct for some items.

1 **It is important to read the job description carefully when preparing for an interview because it will help you ____.**

- **a** deliver an effective presentation about the company during the interview
- **b** answer the employer's questions in the best way possible
- **c** know which of your qualifications the employer is looking for

2 **Researching the job role before the interview can help you ____.**

- **a** decide if the job is something you can and want to do
- **b** discover whether employees like working at the company
- **c** prepare relevant questions to ask during the interview

3 **During an interview, if you are asked an illegal or inappropriate question, you should ____.**

- **a** tell the interviewer that the question is inappropriate
- **b** ask how the question relates to the position
- **c** avoid answering the question by changing the subject

4 **At the end of an interview, you should show confidence by asking the interviewer ____.**

- **a** whether you are a top candidate for the position
- **b** for information about the salary and benefits
- **c** for their opinion about the company's work environment

5 **What should you bring with you to an interview?**

- **a** relevant work samples
- **b** something to take notes with
- **c** a small gift for the interviewer

6 **What are some helpful tips to remember while being interviewed?**

- **a** spend at least 10 minutes answering each question
- **b** make eye contact with your interviewers
- **c** avoid talking about unrelated topics

7 **After the interview, you should follow up by sending ____.**

- **a** an email thanking the interviewers for their time and information
- **b** an email requesting a meeting to discuss how the interview went
- **c** a thank-you email adding information you forgot to say during the interview

8 **Indira is interviewing for a business development manager position at a large tech company. The position is responsible for overseeing the company's marketing initiatives, increasing sales, and helping team members meet goals and develop their skills. The ideal candidate has a degree in business, experience in sales and marketing, and strong communication skills. Which of the following answers is the best way for Indira to respond to this question: *Tell me about yourself*?**

- **a** I've lived in the area for over 20 years and enjoy going to local museums and hiking in the mountains on the weekends.
- **b** I've been interested in marketing since college and enjoy building relationships with colleagues. I also find it exciting to help companies grow.
- **c** I grew up in London and moved here a couple of years ago with my husband. We are passionate about helping others and volunteer at a local food bank.

9 **During Indira's interview for the business development manager position, she is asked, *What's your biggest strength?* Which of the following answers is the best way for Indira to respond to this question?**

- **a** My greatest strength is my ability to connect with colleagues and get their support for new initiatives. My former supervisors often noted how much people trusted and respected my ideas.
- **b** When I was younger, I thought I would be a good teacher because I love working with children. I later realized that I excel in management because I have strong leadership skills.
- **c** I have strong interpersonal communication skills. I also have a lot of experience using different computer software programs.

10 **Indira's interviewer also asked her, *What questions do you have for me?* Which of the following answers is the best way for Indira to respond to this question?**

- **a** Yes, I do have one question. Can you please tell me what benefits are included with this position?
- **b** Yes. Can you please tell me what the company's mission statement is? I didn't have time to look this up.
- **c** Yes, I do. Can you please tell me what you enjoy most about working for this company?

DISCUSSION STRATEGIES

Discussion strategies

When you are in class or at work, you may need to take part in discussions. To successfully participate, you can use a number of different kinds of strategies. They include strategies that help you:

1. Work with others
2. Clarify what you hear or clarify what you say
3. Get and stay involved in the discussion
4. Organize your ideas

During each discussion in class, choose one kind of strategy you want to improve or one you think will be useful. Pick a phrase and try to use it during the in-class activities. Remember to always say the phrase in a polite way.

You can listen to the phrases and examples ▶.

1 Working with others

Some strategies can make it easier to work with other people who are part of the discussion. If you can, try starting the discussion or helping to keep the discussion moving in the right direction. These strategies can help.

Management strategies	Sample phrases
a Starting the discussion	▶ Are we ready to start? ▶ Let's begin.
b Asking others to participate	▶ Who wants to answer first? ▶ Does anyone have anything to add?
c Helping specific people to get involved	▶ Chris, what do you think? ▶ Donna, do you have anything to add?
d Jumping in with talkative people	▶ That's a good point, but let's hear from other people. ▶ Let's hear what everyone else has to say.
e Staying on the topic	▶ That's interesting, but it's a different topic. ▶ Let's finish this point before we talk about that.
f Keeping the discussion moving	▶ Let's move to the next question. ▶ We can talk about that later.
g Telling someone you can't hear them*	▶ I'm sorry. I didn't hear what you said. ▶ Can you speak a little louder?
h Telling someone they speak too fast*	▶ I'm sorry. Can you say that a little slower? ▶ Can you speak more slowly, please?

*You can also use clarification strategies to make sure you understood someone who is quiet or talks too quickly.

2 Clarifying

Sometimes it is hard for you to understand what someone is saying or for others to understand you. Clarifying is a natural part of discussions. Even native speakers use these strategies because not everyone understands everything all the time!

Clarification strategies	Sample phrases	Examples
a Clarifying (when you didn't understand someone else)	▶ I don't understand. ▶ I'm not sure what you mean.	

Discussion strategies

Clarification strategies	Sample phrases	Examples
b Restating (when someone doesn't understand you)	In other words . . . I mean . . .	A: Networking sites can be really helpful. B: I'm sorry? A: In other words, networking sites are useful. A: A good team leader can inspire employees. B: Sorry? A: I mean a good leader can motivate a team.
c Checking (when you want to make sure someone understands you)	Do you see what I mean? Is that clear?	
d Paraphrasing (what the speaker says)	Are you saying that . . . Do you mean that . . .	A: This new software will be more efficient. B: Are you saying that it's faster and easier to use than our current system? A: My team has way too many new projects. B: Do you mean that workload is a problem?
e Paraphrasing (what someone else says)	Lu said that . . . What . . . means is . . .	Lu said that clients have complained. What Kim means is he didn't set any SMART goals.

3 Getting involved

It can be challenging to participate in discussions. Sometimes you have to involve yourself without being asked, keep your turn (if others try to interrupt you), interrupt (when others are talking), and get your turn back (after being interrupted).

Participation strategies	Sample phrases	Examples
a Getting involved	Can I ask a question? I have something I'd like to say.	
b Keeping your turn	Excuse me, I'd just like to finish what I'm saying. I'm just about to finish.	
c Interrupting	Excuse me . . . Sorry to interrupt . . .	Excuse me, but I'd like to add something. Sorry to interrupt, but I have a question.
d Getting your turn back	As I was saying . . . Going back to what I was saying . . .	As I was saying, many companies have a diversity and inclusion plan. Going back to what I was saying, time logs are a good tool to use.
e Commenting (on what someone has said)	That's a good point . . . I see what you mean . . .	That's a good point, Kate. I see what you mean, Sam.
f Adding (to what someone has said)	I agree with you . . . and also . . . Another thing to consider is . . .	I agree with you, Mia, and also, we need to improve time management. Yes, and another thing to consider is productivity.

Discussion strategies

4 Organizing

Lastly, organization techniques can help communication and make discussion easier to follow.

Organization techniques	Sample words and phrases	Examples
a Chronological	First . . . second . . . third . . . Next . . . then . . . later	▶ First, let's talk about the scenario. Second, let's share our ideas. Third, let's suggest ideas. ▶ Next, we will talk about some ideas for this proposal. Then, we'll work on it as a team. Later, we'll get together and share our work.
b Cause and effect	If . . . , then . . . When . . . then . . .	▶ If you use SMART goals, then you are more likely to succeed. ▶ When we finish this task, then we can go onto the next.
c Categorical	There are three categories . . . The main characteristics . . .	▶ There are three categories of user for this technology: beginner, intermediate, and expert. ▶ These are the main characteristics that make someone a good leader.
d Problem and solution	The best solution is . . . That way . . .	▶ The best solution is to form teams so that we get more ideas. ▶ Let's talk to the manager and that way we can discuss the issue face-to-face.
e Comparison	Also . . . In the same way . . .	▶ Networking sites are good places to look for jobs. Also, you can use those sites to meet people from other companies. ▶ Our physical health is important. In the same way, emotional wellness is essential for a balanced lifestyle.
f Contrast	Although . . . However . . .	▶ Although working in teams is important, being able to work independently is a valuable skill. ▶ The candidate doesn't have a lot of experience in this industry. However, she is a great fit for our company.

VOCABULARY PRACTICE

Vocabulary practice 1

Exercise (A)

Complete the puzzle. What is the vertical word?

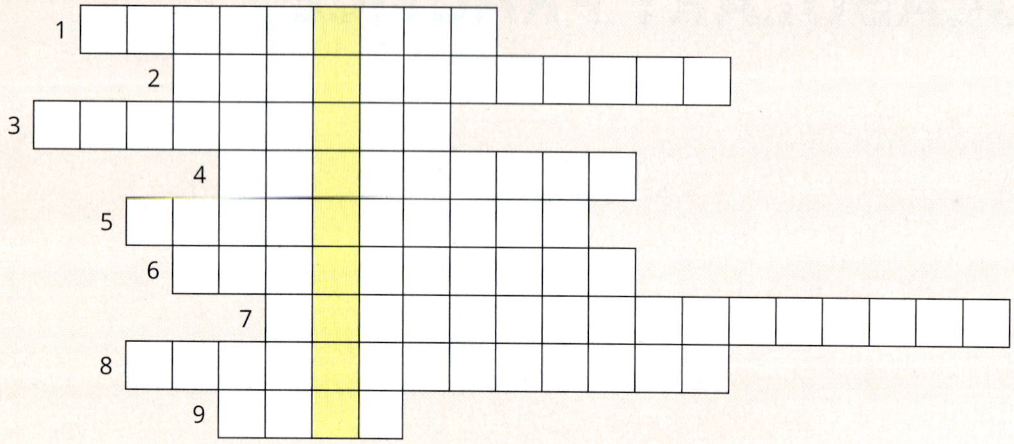

1 Comments pointing to problems or mistakes: ____________ *that was hard to accept*
2 Easy to go talk to, sociable: *a very* ____________ *boss*
3 Behaving as if you're fighting back against negative comments: *listen without getting* ____________
4 Feeling a strong reason to do something: ____________ *to improve*
5 Communicating respect: *speaking in a* ____________ *way*
6 The idea you have about a person or thing based on what you see or hear: *make a good first* ____________
7 A bad situation resulting from a problem in communication: *the need to avoid any* ____________
8 Being ready with the skills you need to get a job: *ways to improve your* ____________
9 The attitude or feeling your voice shows: *spoken with a professional* ____________

Exercise (B)

Use the correct words from the puzzle to complete the conversations.

1

She seems highly 1 ____________ to succeed.

Yes, she made that 2 ____________ on me, too.

2

My idea got some 3 ____________ but also lots of positive feedback.

I hope you didn't get 4 ____________ about any negative comments.

3

You know, better communication skills would increase your 5 ____________.

That's true. For one thing, my emails need a more professional 6 ____________.

4

Is the new sales manager 7 ____________?

Yes, he's very 8 ____________ and kind to all his team.

Vocabulary practice 2

Exercise A

Read the clues and find the words.

U	T	S	U	C	C	E	S	S	F	U	L	L	Y
E	V	R	P	N	I	Z	J	R	R	A	S	O	T
E	D	E	A	L	W	I	T	H	Q	G	G	M	H
S	O	S	J	E	I	A	I	B	N	T	U	X	A
S	C	O	M	M	A	N	D	Z	U	S	I	R	N
B	V	L	B	A	F	L	E	H	R	Z	D	O	K
I	B	V	P	H	A	O	N	G	E	I	E	L	G
O	R	E	S	P	E	C	T	F	U	L	L	Y	O
N	M	W	D	X	H	U	I	M	M	S	I	J	O
T	Q	C	U	L	N	S	F	T	I	G	N	C	D
R	U	N	L	A	T	E	Y	L	W	F	E	Y	N
I	N	T	E	R	A	C	T	I	O	N	S	K	E
V	R	D	A	S	X	A	C	K	Y	E	X	E	S
S	E	M	B	A	R	R	A	S	S	I	N	G	S

1 Let's check the ____________ for instructions on how to do this.

2 That wasn't a request; it was a ____________.

3 It is a good idea to ____________ problems quickly rather than ignore them.

4 It's important to treat both customers and employees ____________.

5 Everyone congratulated me on completing my training ____________.

6 Let's sit down, talk, and try to ____________ this disagreement.

7 Remain calm and polite in all your ____________ with clients.

8 The first step is to ____________ what the problem is; then we can work on solving it.

Exercise B

Use the correct words from the puzzle to complete an employee's notes from a meeting.

MEETING NOTES

- *Treatment of customers (external and internal):*

  Remember to follow department 1 ____________.

  Always treat customers and co-workers 2 ____________.

- *Handling problems:*

  3 ____________ *problems right away—don't delay.*

  Stay calm and keep all 4 ____________ *professional.*

- *Communication skills:*

  Make polite requests—avoid 5 ____________.

  6 ____________ *ways I can improve.*

Vocabulary practice 3

Exercise A

Complete the puzzle. What is the vertical word?

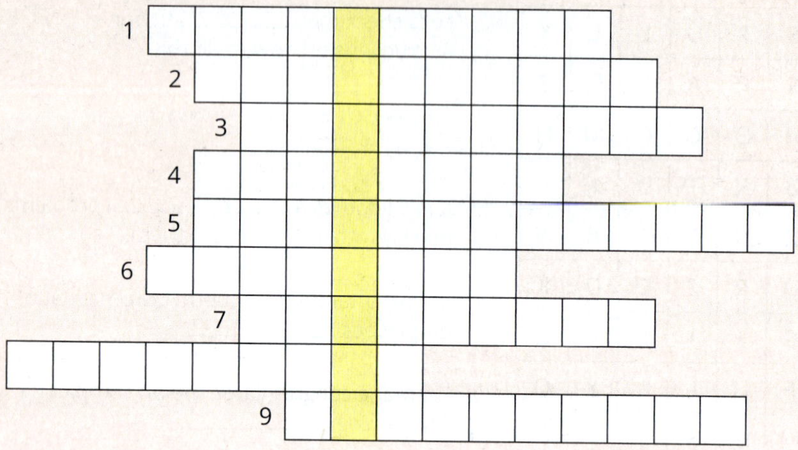

1 If you are able to do this to a job on your list, then you have succeeded in doing it.
2 If you have this kind of goal, then it is possible.
3 If you compare one thing with others, then you consider it in this way.
4 If you have this kind of experience, then it's clearly related to what you're doing.
5 If you think carefully about something, then you give it this.
6 If you have goals of this kind, then you're planning far into the future.
7 If you have goals of this kind, then you're planning for the near future.
8 If you must finish a project by a deadline, then it's this kind of project.
9 If you want to be able to tell how well you're doing, then your progress should be like this.

Exercise B

Use the correct words from the puzzle to complete the employee's notes to himself.

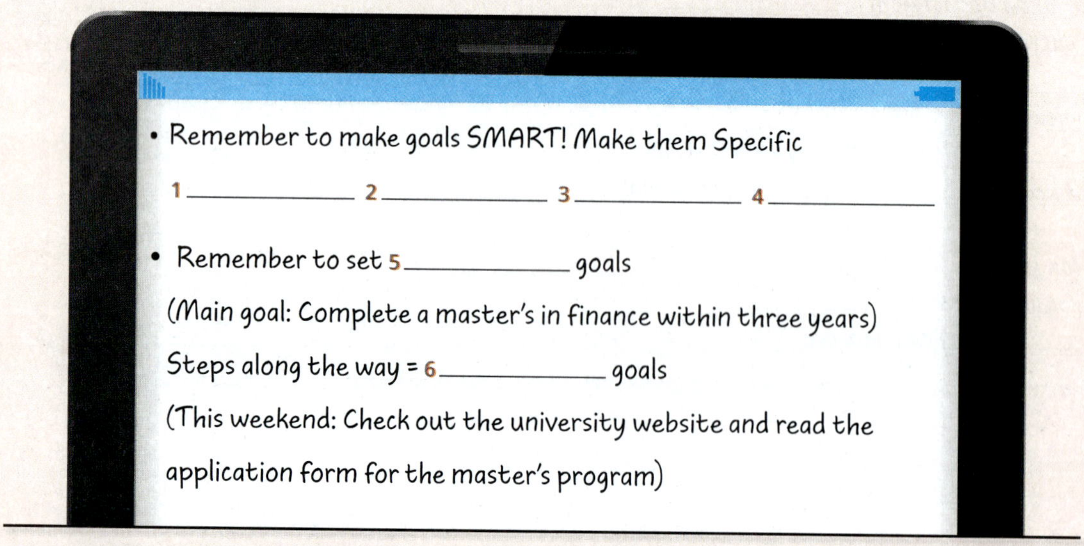

Vocabulary practice 4

Exercise A

Complete the puzzle.

Across

2 to reach the result you want by working hard

5 happening without a break

7 to help cause something you want to happen

8 a quality that makes a person or something different from others

9 special attention given to a person because of something good they've done

10 the way something is organized, arranged, or built

Down

1 producing the result you planned or wanted

3 the duty to take care of something

4 the power to give orders to people

6 to work with others in order to get something done

Exercise B

Use the correct words from the puzzle to complete a manager's email to her team.

Email

Jackie Lee, Director of Operations

To: Everyone

Subject: Off to a great start!

Dear team,

I just want to tell you all how pleased I am with the new organization of the department. Our new team 1 ______________ is already working well. I've seen individuals 2 ______________ as a team and share 3 ______________ for completing the work. It makes me proud, and I'm sure it's going to make us more 4 ______________. You all deserve 5 ______________ for the way you've accepted the changes and worked hard to 6 ______________ our goals. Keep up the good work!

Vocabulary practice 5

Exercise (A)

Complete the puzzle.

Across

3 You want to meet at 8:00; I'd prefer 10:00. Let's __________ on 9:00, OK?

5 A successful team must have good communication. It's __________.

8 We must resolve this __________ before we can move ahead with the project.

9 Let's work together to __________ the problem and think of a solution.

Down

1 Let's try looking at the problem from a different __________.

2 It's __________ for me when my team members won't listen to my ideas.

4 We share the same __________. We both believe in being honest and responsible.

5 What a great imagination you have! You make such __________ suggestions.

6 How about some team-building exercises? They can be especially __________ for new staff.

7 Her pleasant __________ makes her easy to work with.

Exercise (B)

Use the correct words from the puzzle to complete the conversations.

1

How did your team think of that solution? It's so 1 __________!

It helped that each of us had our own 2 __________ on the problem.

2

It's very beneficial that each member of this team has a different 3 __________, don't you think?

Yes, it's great! I'd even call it 4 __________.

3

I'm sorry to hear that your team had a major 5 __________.

It's fine. We were able to 6 __________ and complete the project.

4

I find it hard to work with him. At times, it's really 7 __________.

Yes, I can see that. You two care about different things. You have different 8 __________.

Vocabulary practice 6

Exercise (A)

Read the clues and find the words and phrases.

A	A	C	K	N	O	W	L	E	D	G	E	E	B	C
R	E	W	A	R	D	M	V	C	B	J	W	V	K	O
R	O	C	Q	Y	F	F	I	D	P	F	V	I	I	L
E	V	O	U	I	N	Z	T	K	O	X	Q	S	N	L
B	L	M	A	H	I	B	A	O	W	W	S	I	S	A
R	A	E	L	K	J	N	L	X	E	O	Z	O	P	B
R	Q	U	I	I	Q	M	M	S	R	D	Z	N	I	O
O	U	P	T	E	N	C	O	U	R	A	G	E	R	R
L	X	W	Y	T	A	K	E	P	A	R	T	H	E	A
E	E	I	Y	W	B	A	B	K	S	X	C	Q	G	T
M	T	T	S	U	P	E	R	V	I	S	I	O	N	I
O	K	H	H	A	P	R	O	M	O	T	I	O	N	V
D	U	P	S	X	I	E	A	U	Z	C	G	B	D	E
E	J	L	R	H	W	T	A	K	E	A	R	I	S	K
L	E	A	D	E	R	S	H	I	P	H	O	L	C	M

1 To think of, invent: ____________ *a solution*

2 To do something that may not be safe: *warned me not to* ____________

3 An idea or plan: *his* ____________ *for the future of the company*

4 A person whom others respect and copy: *serve as a* ____________ *for younger staff*

5 Management, direction: *working under her* ____________

6 Essential: ____________ *to our success*

7 To give someone the desire to do something well; to motivate: ____________ *your staff to work harder*

8 To give credit to: *publicly* ____________ *your team members for their work*

9 To try to persuade someone to feel more confident or take action: ____________ *them to be more creative*

10 A move up: *reward an employee with a* ____________

Exercise (B)

Use the correct words from the puzzle to complete an advertisement for a leadership course.

Leadership Course **Starting Soon!**

Northern University School of Business

Are you ready to move into a position of greater responsibility?

This well-known program will help you develop skills that are 1 ____________ for any leader in the business world.

Learn how to

- make smarter decisions
- communicate your 2 ____________ for the future
- become a 3 ____________ for your colleagues
- 4 ____________ others to do their best, especially when they're without direct 5 ____________

See what recent graduates of our program have to say. Our Leadership Course has played a valuable role in their careers, helping each get a 6 ____________ and achieve their goals.

REGISTER NOW!

Vocabulary practice 7

Exercise A

Complete the puzzle.

Across

5 If you guess something is less than it actually is, you do this.

6 If you're working on something important, avoid letting anyone or anything do this.

9 If you have topics to discuss at a meeting, put them on this.

10 If you guess something is more than it actually is, you do this.

Down

1 If you improve this, you increase how fast goods or services are produced.

2 If you can't measure an exact amount or number, do this as a best guess.

3 If you work in a way that wastes no time, money, or energy, you're being this.

4 If you have a duty to make something happen and to explain your actions, then you're this.

7 If something is absolutely necessary, then it's this.

8 If something is important and should get your attention, then make it this.

Exercise B

Use the correct words from the puzzle to complete the statements in the questionnaire. Then check the boxes that are true for you.

Are *YOU* Working SMART?

Read the statements and check your answers.	Strongly agree	Agree	Disagree	Strongly disagree
1 I don't **1** ________ my work to keep checking my email.	☐	☐	☐	☐
2 I'm usually correct when I **2** ________ how long work will take.	☐	☐	☐	☐
3 I don't waste time on things that aren't a **3** ________.	☐	☐	☐	☐
4 I attend meetings only when they are really **4** ________.	☐	☐	☐	☐
5 I'm as fast and **5** ________ as possible in the way I do my job.	☐	☐	☐	☐
6 I'm happy with my level of **6** ________ and so is my manager.	☐	☐	☐	☐

Vocabulary practice 8

Exercise (A)

Complete the puzzle. What is the vertical word?

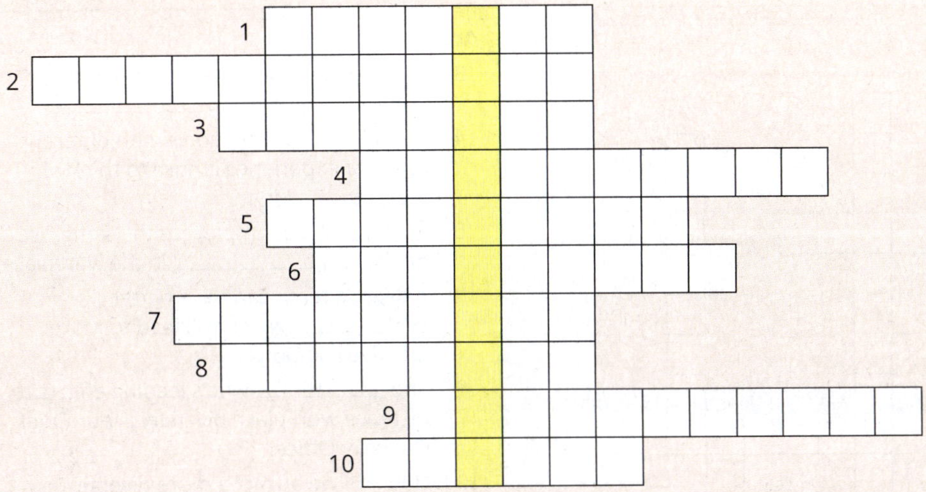

1 to give different things the correct level of importance compared to one another
2 relating to the mind and the ability to think
3 alone, apart from other people
4 to make something stronger, better, or more effective
5 relating to beliefs and feelings about life rather than physical things
6 connected with or related to feelings
7 an aspect, element, or part of something
8 how much work someone has to do
9 the sense of being happy with what you are doing
10 to make a judgement about something after thinking carefully

Exercise (B)

Use the correct words from the puzzle to complete the conversations.

1

I notice you always bring a 1 ___________ lunch to work.

I do now. A while ago, I decided to 2 ___________ my diet, and I saw that I had to improve it.

2

I think a person's 3 ___________ health really depends on good relationships.

Yes! And we should spend more time with friends to 4 ___________ those relationships.

3

Are you able to 5 ___________ your work life and your personal life?

I try, but my increasing 6 ___________ is keeping me at work longer!

4

He seems so calm and happy, like he has a real sense of 7 ___________.

Maybe it's because of his charity work and his 8 ___________ life.

Vocabulary practice 9

Exercise (A)

Complete the puzzle.

Across

3 My boss not only talks about diversity, she's working hard to __________ it.

4 A team of creative people with different areas of experience is sure to think of __________ ideas.

6 We treat all our employees the same. We don't accept __________ in the workplace.

8 A diverse team can have better __________, which will lead to more creative solutions.

9 The __________ who's leading efforts to increase workplace diversity is our Chief Diversity Officer.

10 How will we attract a more diverse workforce? What's our __________?

Down

1 Actions caused by __________ or other negative views do a lot of damage in the workplace.

2 We're hoping that education will lead to greater __________ of differences.

5 It is part of the company's __________ to create an inclusive workplace.

7 Our CEO believes in diversity but isn't sure how to __________ a diversity program.

Exercise (B)

Use the correct words from the puzzle to complete an email from a CEO to her Chief Diversity Officer.

Email

MJ Johnson
To: Amina Abdi
Subject: News

Hi Amina,

Great news! We are about to be named one of the "Best Places to Work" on the *City Times* list. The story will be out tomorrow, but I couldn't wait to thank you for working so hard to 1 __________ diversity in our workforce. It's a big reason we made the list. You have succeeded in thinking of new and 2 __________ methods to attract and keep great employees, and the 3 __________ you are using to do this is clearly the correct one. As a result, we are succeeding as a company in our 4 __________ to stop 5 __________ in the workplace. In all of your work, you have shown a spirit of 6 __________ toward your colleagues that makes you a role model for us all.

Many thanks! Mary Jane

Vocabulary practice 10

Exercise A

Read the clues and find the words and phrases.

B	A	S	O	L	I	T	U	D	E	G	E	A	B	M
R	S	W	A	P	O	U	T	F	I	T	W	V	C	A
O	T	C	Q	Y	F	F	I	D	P	F	V	I	O	T
E	A	O	U	N	I	Q	U	E	O	X	Q	S	M	H
B	N	S	U	I	T	A	B	I	L	I	T	Y	P	E
N	D	E	L	K	J	N	L	X	A	O	Z	O	E	M
O	O	D	E	D	I	C	A	T	E	D	J	E	T	A
V	U	P	T	E	N	C	O	U	R	A	W	X	I	T
E	T	W	Y	A	T	K	E	P	V	R	Y	P	T	I
L	E	I	Y	W	B	A	B	K	S	X	M	E	I	C
N	A	M	B	I	T	I	O	U	S	V	A	R	V	I
G	K	A	U	T	H	E	N	T	I	C	G	T	E	A
D	U	P	S	X	I	E	A	U	Z	C	I	I	D	N
C	O	M	B	I	N	A	T	I	O	N	C	S	N	W
K	L	E	X	D	E	R	S	Q	I	P	H	E	C	K

1 If a person or thing is one of a kind, unlike anyone or anything else, then this word describes them.

2 If you have special skills in an area or know a lot about it, then you have this.

3 If many people or companies are trying to win something, then the situation is like this.

4 If you have a strong desire to reach big goals, then this word describes you.

5 If two or more things happen or work together, then they form one of these.

6 If people or things really are what they're said to be, then they're this.

7 If you do this, it means people notice you, usually because you're good at something.

8 If you want to get a job you're applying for, you must persuade the company that you have this.

Exercise B

Use the correct words from the puzzle to complete the statements in the self-test. Then choose the answers that are true for you.

Oceanside Graduate School of Business

A message from the **Career Center** to all students:
Are *YOU* ready to begin your job search? Test yourself! Circle your answers to these statements

I know just how 1 ______ the job market is in my chosen field.	Yes	No	Not Sure
I know how to 2 ______ from the crowd of job hunters.	Yes	No	Not Sure
I know how to build a personal brand that is 3 ______.	Yes	No	Not Sure
My personal brand is a 4 ______ of my skills, personality, and values.	Yes	No	Not Sure
I know what new skills and areas of 5 ______ I want to develop.	Yes	No	Not Sure
I am open and honest, so interviewers see me as 6 ______.	Yes	No	Not Sure
People call me 7 ______ because I set big goals for myself.	Yes	No	Not Sure

Did you answer *No* or *Not sure* in some cases?
Would you like some job search coaching?
Sign up here for an appointment with a Career Center staff member.

Vocabulary practice 11

Exercise A

Complete the puzzle.

Across

2 a group of people who know and help each other, often because they do the same kind of work

3 to make something better

8 people that have earned a degree or diploma from a university or other school

10 a written statement that a person is a good choice to be given a job or be accepted by a school, etc.

11 to have a sociable conversation about common, everyday topics

Down

1 happening or existing on computers only (not in the real world)

4 to make something bigger

5 to continue spoken or written communication with someone, whether often or only rarely

6 the ideas and opinion that people have about a person, based on what has happened in the past

7 a short description with important details about who a person is

9 people that you communicate with, whether speaking or writing to them

Exercise B

Use the correct words from the puzzle to complete someone's notes from a talk about career development.

10/28, 9:00 a.m. "Getting Ahead" w/ Terry Jones, Chris Lee

- Reasons to build a professional 1 ______________:
  To share info
  To support each other
  To have people who can give you a 2 ______________ when you're job hunting

- Successful people have lots of 3 ______________, so try to meet new people IRL.
  Then remember to 4 ______________ with them (via social media, emailing, etc.)

  (Talking to new people is hard—I hate to 5 ______________—how can I get better at it?)

- To do:
  1 Attend a 6 ______________ networking event (See schedule of online events for Appleton Univ. alumni)
  2 Take another look at the personal 7 ______________ I posted online. Is it good enough, or can I 8 ______________ it in any way?

Vocabulary practice 12

Exercise (A)

Complete the puzzle. What is the vertical word?

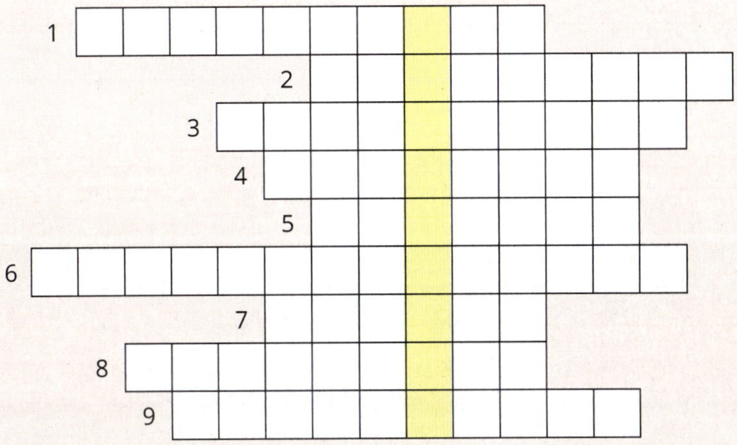

1 The company is looking for someone with a ____________ in public relations.
2 A ____________ must make a good impression on the interviewers to be successful.
3 You'll need to give the company the names and contact information of your ____________.
4 Tell the interviewer about the experience you've had that's most ____________ to the position.
5 In this country, it's ____________ for an interviewer to ask your age.
6 Your résumé shows that you have all the right ____________ for the position.
7 Gender should not be a ____________ in deciding who gets the job.
8 After a job interview, it's hard to wait for the company's decision, but don't get ____________.
9 You would be great at that job! You should go into the interview with ____________.

Exercise (B)

Use the correct words from the puzzle to complete the conversations.

1

Which 1 ____________ do you think will get the job?

The last one. She's got all the right 2 ____________ and good social skills, too.

2

The company asked for three 3 ____________, but I gave them only two names.

Well, I hope that won't be a 4 ____________ in their decision.

3

I have a lot of work experience, but some of it is 5 ____________ to the position.

That's OK. In your interview, just focus on your most 6 ____________ skills.

4

They're looking for someone with a strong 7 ____________ in computer science.

That's you! You can talk with 8 ____________ about all your experience.

GLOSSARY

Glossary

Module 1: Communication 1

donate (v) to give money to an organization that needs help
fund (n) an organization that is responsible for collecting and spending money for a particular purpose
gesture (n) a movement of your hands, arms, or head that shows what you mean or how you feel

Module 2: Communication 2

embarrassing (adj) making you feel worried and unhappy about what other people will think of you
run late* (phr) to arrive, go somewhere, or do something late
thank goodness* (phr) said to show that you are very glad about something

Module 3: Goal Setting

cut (n) a reduction in the amount or price of something
sample (n) a small amount of a product that people can try in order to find out what it is like

Module 4: Teamwork

booth (n) a small place, especially outdoors, where you can buy something or get information, for example at a fair
chip in (phr v) to give money, help, advice, etc. to add to what other people are giving
hand out (phr v) to give something to everyone in a group

Module 5: Critical Thinking

campaign (n) a series of things that you do in order to persuade people to do something
compromise (n) an agreement in which both people or groups accept something different from what they wanted at the beginning

Module 6: Leadership

apply (v) to affect, or be true for, a particular person or thing
chancellor (n) the leader of the government in some countries
justice (n) a judge in a law court, for example in the Federal Supreme Court of the U.S.
Supreme Court (n) the most important court in the country or in a state

Module 7: Self-Management

favor (n) something that you do for someone in order to help or to be kind to him or her
grant (n) an amount of money given to a person or organization especially by the government, for a particular purpose
hardware (n) computer equipment and machinery
maintain (v) to take care of something so that it stays in good condition
software (n) the programs that tell a computer how to do a particular job

Module 8: Wellness

grumpy* (adj) a grumpy person gets annoyed easily and does not seem happy
snack (v) to eat small amounts of food between main meals or instead of a meal

Module 9: Social Responsibility

be trapped (phr) to not be able to escape from a bad place or situation
icebreaker (n) something that you say or do to make people less nervous when they first meet
intern (n) someone, especially a student, who works for a short time in a particular job

Module 10: Branding

calculation (n) if you do a calculation, you use mathematics to find a number or amount
dedicated (adj) someone who is dedicated works very hard at something because it is important to them
magic (n) a special power that makes strange or impossible things happen in stories
mathematician (n) someone who has studied mathematics to a high level or who teaches mathematics
novel (n) a book in which the story, characters, and events are not real
outfit (n) a set of clothes worn together
programmer (n) someone whose job is writing programs for computers
programming (n) the act or job of writing instructions for a computer
solitude (n) the state of being alone, usually because you want to be

Module 11: Job Search

company culture (phr) the way people in a company think and behave
meetup (n) an informal meeting or social event

Module 12: Interviewing

nervous* (adj) worried or afraid about something, and unable to relax
on the spot* (phr) immediately, without careful planning
prevent (v) to stop something from happening, or stop someone from doing something

* in audio

Notes

Notes